A powerful exposé on our school system and a true story, 19 years in the making, of how one boy's academic struggles led to his success, in spite of his...

unREAL Education:
Beyond Report Cards

As told by his mother,
Elaine Mellon

(A portion of the proceeds from book sales is being donated to Everyone Reading, NY and the International Dyslexia Association.)

T0147679

A powerful exposé on our school system and a
true story, 19 years in the making, of how one
boy's academic struggles led to his success,
in spite of his...

unREAL Education:
Beyond Report Cards

Elaine Mellon

authorHOUSE®

AuthorHouse™
1663 Liberty Drive
Bloomington, IN 47403
www.authorhouse.com
Phone: 1-800-839-8640

Published by AuthorHouse 2/28/2012

ISBN: 978-1-4685-5504-2 (sc)
ISBN: 978-1-4685-5497-7 (hc)
ISBN: 978-1-4685-5959-0 (e)

Library of Congress Control Number: 2012903038

This book is printed on acid-free paper.

CONTENTS

DEDICATION

This book is dedicated first and foremost to my son, who overcame countless obstacles, despite an education system that failed him. While writing this book, Blake (as I will refer to him) grew into a successful, compassionate young adult.

I would also like to dedicate this book to my family and friends, who stood by and supported me while I persisted in my fight for fairness on Blake's behalf.

I am extremely grateful to my husband and daughters, for all their help and especially, for being the voice of reason, when everything seemed out of control. I also want my family to know how proud I am of them and everything they have accomplished.

FOREWORD

Blake spent most of his academic career being told he was lazy; he was not focusing, he was not paying attention, and he wasn't concentrating. He was told he would do better in school, if he attended extra help more often. According to many teachers and administrators (the educational professionals), it was Blake's fault he was not succeeding.

This is Blake's story; his struggles through school, the hoops he was made to jump through, the negativity he had to deal with, and the incompetence of a school district, that ran rampant. In addition, his story will also include those occasional bright lights that kept him going, along the way.

It was extremely difficult for my family and friends to understand why I was so passionate about helping Blake, even though I was not sure why he was struggling. It was a strong gut feeling (maybe a Mother's intuition!) that something was not right. We were missing a huge piece of the puzzle and no one seemed to have any answers. My family and friends put up with a lot; long phone conversations, my constant battles with teachers and administrators, Blake's temper tantrums when he was younger, with frustrations when he got older, and fights with my husband as to whether or not the school or I was right.

Since Blake entered middle school, I was told, literally dozens of times by his teachers, "Blake must advocate for himself. He needs to be able to come and talk to us. He will need to do this when he goes to college." Blake has been hearing this since he was 12!

There are many things students can't handle themselves, nor should they have to. There are also many teachers that don't want to deal with parents (despite a supposed "Open Door Policy") because many students, especially the younger ones, will do as they are told and not question their teachers.

I felt it was important to write this book for my son. I want him to know how proud I am. I wanted to put his story down on paper so it will help others. My phone rings often with parents asking for help, advice, suggestions and some direction.

Though this is primarily Blake's story, it can't be written without my perspective. I refused to give up on him when everyone else, including some of his teachers (and even Blake himself), was ready to write him off. This is an intimate view of our journey, the highs and lows, through the school system both separately and together.

Please Take Note

The names of those contained in this project have been changed for obvious privacy reasons. However, when initials are used, they are the actual person's initials. I intentionally wanted those people to know how grateful we are and what they have meant to our family.

There will be readers skeptical of some of the issues discussed in this book. Be assured, I have detailed notes, emails, recordings, court testimony, and thousands of pages of documentation to support it all.

1

A Brief Family History

While I was in the process of writing this book, I turned 50. I am living in the house I grew up in, so my children have also attended the same Elementary, Middle, and High School. As you can imagine, it has been a bit surreal at times, especially when some of my teachers are still teaching. Imagine requesting your child not have a certain teacher because you sat in their class 35 years ago. I thought some of them were old and boring back then!

This is the only home I have ever known, except for college, post-college and before getting married. My parents, Blake's maternal grandparents, are Snow Birds and live with us four to six months a year.

Charles and I have been married 27 years. At this time, Blake is 19, his sister, Michelle, is 24 and his other sister, Nicole, is now 22. Most of our extended families live in relatively close proximity to us, so we see a lot of each other.

My husband has been with the same company for over 25 years and I have always worked part time, mostly in the fitness industry.

One of the most ironic choices I have made over the years was NOT to move. My husband and my children have all expressed interest in moving at some point. For years, I strongly resisted. After all, we live in one of the best school systems in the country. Of course, they will be able to help us with Blake. If we move, I don't know what we'll get. At least here, I know the people. I know the system. Blake will thrive.

To quote from Paul Anka and Frank Sinatra, "Regrets, I have a few..." Along with "Regrets", there is also a lot of sadness, anger, passion, and motivation to do what you feel is right.

2

FROM THE BEGINNING: IT'S A BOY!

Blake was born, the last of my three children, on a rainy Wednesday morning, in June of 1992. I was in labor for 11 hours and in terrible back pain. When the doctor suggested an epidural, I jumped at the chance. After having two girls the "natural" way, I was so ready to try something different. How wonderful it was. Five minutes before Blake was born, I was talking to my sister-in-law on the phone, pain free. The downside was that I was not able to push, so they needed to suction him out. I have always felt somewhat guilty about that.

Everything seemed fine. He was a beautiful boy, blonde; blue eyed, 7 pounds, 14 ounces, 21 inches long. I did not know I was having a boy. I wanted to be surprised. After having my girls, I was convinced he was a girl. I had no boy names picked out. Later, to my surprise, my husband admitted he had called the doctor, a few weeks earlier, to inquire about the gender. He kept that secret from everyone.

They took Blake from me to clean him up, as I was in need of sleep. This next part is a bit of a blur, but at some point the doctor came in and told me they moved Blake to the NICU! They thought there might be something wrong with his palate. He was not sucking like he should. I was still really out of it and actually slept through the night.

I woke up early the next morning and my pediatrician was at my bedside making his rounds. [I must digress for a moment and talk about Dr. Dan. This man was my doctor since I was born! He took care of my sister and me and then continued to take care of our children. He even made house calls early on. You never waited more than five minutes in his office. His diagnostic skills were second to none. I truly love this man.]

Dr. Dan asked if I wanted to go in and see Blake. Of course, I said yes. He then proceeded with some words of caution, "Blake is still in NICU and he is in an incubator. There are many tubes attached to his body and you will only be able to touch him with the attached gloves. One more thing, he will have to stay in the hospital a few days after you go home."

I listened to what he said but it did not register. All I kept thinking was that my husband was not going to be there, for at least another hour. I did not want to wait to see my son. Still sore from the episiotomy, the doctor and I walked slowly to the NICU. I was not prepared for what I saw as we approached the door.

We got to the door and the nurse came over and handed me a gown, hat, and covers for my slippers. As I was getting dressed, the doctor pointed to one of the incubators where Blake was laying so still. In an instant, my knees became so weak; I collapsed into Dr. Dan's arms. I felt sick. I could not stop crying. He held me so tight. I will always be grateful to him for that.

Blake was in the hospital for a total of five days, the longest five days of my life! It is just not right to leave your newborn in the hospital.

Fortunately, everything turned out okay. Blake's palate was fine. His sucking was strong and surgery was not needed. Dr. Dan cleared him to come home.

3

Blake's Story: The Start Of His Academic Career (Pre-K through 5)

Blake's troubles, with school, begin here. Included, will be his comments to me, my comments to his teachers and involved professionals, suggestions made by all involved, and comments on the ideas that did and did not work.

At this point in time, I am writing out of frustration. The district has recommended the same interventions for this year as last. Last year was a disaster. I have been repeating, for the last few years, to anyone who will listen, that we are all missing a major piece to this puzzle, to help Blake achieve success. We need to find answers...

<u>PRE-KINDERGARTEN</u>

Blake was a normal, active, four year old. He has been riding a two-wheeler since before he turned three! He is happiest when he is throwing a ball around and loves being outside. His favorite TV shows are Barney, Power Rangers, Popular Mechanics for Kids (PMK), and SportsCenter.

He loves being read to, but has no interest in learning his letters or his numbers. He can't write his name and doesn't even want to attempt it. He does however know the "ABC Song", can make change when we go to the store, knows all the street names to get to school and many other places.

4

Blake has been in pre-school since he was three. The first year, it was two mornings a week and the second year, it was three. By the end of pre-school, Blake was finally starting to write his name, but not very well. His attempt at letters and numbers was weak at best.

You are always told you should never compare your children. How could I not? My oldest was reading before she was in Kindergarten and my other daughter was reading in Kindergarten. Both wrote their letters beautifully. I just thought that it was different because Blake was an active, June, baby boy!

KINDERGARTEN

Blake was excited about starting Kindergarten. His teacher, Ms. McCarry, was wonderful. In fact, it was she that approached us and said she is observing something about Blake, but is not sure, if it is developmental or something else.

He still had trouble writing. His letters and numbers were not smooth; sometimes some of the letters were backwards and sometimes not. He would write from the bottom up. He still was not reading. It was recommended he be given speech classes once a week. He loved working on puzzles, looking through "I Spy" books and also loved anything to do with money. He and his dad would play these adding and subtracting games in the car. Anything to do with numbers was attractive to him. One of his favorite games was "The Memory Game", a modern version of "Concentration".

FIRST GRADE

This was a difficult year right from the start. Blake continued with Speech through the first half of the year. So many negative things happened in school. I will break it down by category, subject, or event in order to explain.

Spelling: For the first 2½ months of school, Blake could not pass a single spelling test. He also couldn't read the weekly sight words. One day, out of nowhere, I had this revelation. Blake's teacher, Mrs. Aroyo, came from a different elementary school that used different teaching methods. She wrote their sight words in Denelian letter formation (very curly), not block letters. I brought this to the attention of the Principal, Ms. Peel, and she had Mrs. Aroyo change her word list immediately. Mrs. Aroyo was not happy with me.

Reading: Blake still was not reading and had no interest. Everyone was in agreement that his math skills were strong. I approached the teacher with the idea that we "fake" him into reading by giving him math problems or puzzles. She looked at me like I had three heads! Instead, he was recommended for the remedial reading program.

Discipline Problem: Mrs. Aroyo, very quickly into the year, labeled Blake as a discipline problem. She would repeatedly call me at home to tell me he would not follow directions and he would not stay in his seat.

There was one episode when she called and told me Blake threw a tissue box at one of the girls and that he refused to apologize. At this point, I had had enough of this teacher. I told her this didn't sound like Blake at all. He wouldn't throw something at any girl and she was a good friend of his. I told her I would talk to him when he got home.

When Blake got home, he was angry and upset. He told me he didn't throw anything, that the teacher yelled at him in front of everyone. She was mad at him for not apologizing, but he was not going to apologize for something he didn't do. (It is important to know the girl was not hurt.)

Again I had a flash. Mrs. Aroyo never asked Blake what he did or why he did it. I asked Blake what happened because it dawned on me that what she saw might not have been exactly what she thought she saw.

Blake was sitting at a "table" with 4-6 desks pushed together so everyone is facing in different directions. There was, in fact, a tissue box, on the table, that was angled on two different desk heights. Blake was not facing the board and, at this point in time, was more fascinated with the tissue box than whatever the teacher was teaching. He began to tap the underside of the box where it made a small triangle. At some point, he tapped it too strongly and flipped the box. It ended up in the girl's lap! The teacher yelled at him for "throwing" the box and she wouldn't listen to him when he tried to explain. From then on, Blake shut down in her class and basically lost all of 1st grade. His only saving grace was happily "escaping" to the Reading teacher.

I explained to my son that even though he didn't mean to hit anyone, he did. He is responsible so he should apologize to her. He apologized but made sure Mrs. Aroyo knew he did not "throw" the box at his friend!

Blake is very literal and some things need to be explained or expanded. As for him not paying attention or getting out of his seat, we figured out why in second grade, after I insisted on having him tested.

Blake's favorite game continued to be Memory and constructing his matchbox racing tracks. He also enjoyed setting up the dominoes. He even learned to play chess.

One interesting observation came from the Reading teacher. She said he was holding the pencil too tight and had him start using pencil cushions! Blake had reading once a week for about a ½ hour in a group setting.

SECOND GRADE

The Principal and I hand picked Blake's teacher for 2nd grade. It was a teacher that my oldest daughter had. Mrs. Birdie was organized, strict yet fair. Blake already had a rapport with her because of his sister. He continued with the remedial reading program.

He appeared to be making some progress in becoming more enthusiastic about school. He was not even on a first grade reading level yet, for what I thought were obvious reasons.

A few months into school, Blake came home and asked if I could talk to Mrs. Birdie about him not reading aloud in class. The whole class reads out loud together and by the time he figures out the word, he can't find where everyone else is! He is now only seven, very verbal, in fact, more verbal than his peers. I casually mentioned it to the teacher.

A few weeks later, she called me very concerned. Blake failed his social studies test. I was stunned. I studied with him and he knew everything. How could this be?

A few weeks after that, she called again and was happy because he got a 90 on his science test. This didn't make any sense. He failed his social studies test but did so well on the science? I made an appointment to come in and see the tests. For the science test, the multiple-choice answers were pictures and they had taken a practice test the day before. He basically memorized the pictures. The one question Blake got wrong was the only one not on the practice test.

I felt something was not right and I asked to have Blake tested. The Principal and School Psychologist actually tried to discourage me by saying that even though Blake was on the young side; he was "progressing nicely". I insisted he be tested.

I believe it was February by the time the testing was completed by the School Psychologist, Mrs. Mack. Blake seemed to like her at first and didn't mind playing the games she had him play. Based on the testing and input from his previous teachers (keep in mind his 1st grade teacher), I was told he was showing "signs and symptoms of ADHD" and the "possibility of medication should be explored". I was also told he is strong in math, but very weak in reading and writing. He has processing issues, and has a short-term memory problem. Once the information is in his long-term memory, he gets it! If he is verbally given a list of things to do, he will probably do the first one, maybe the second, but it would be like he never even heard the third. This was the problem he had with his 1st grade teacher. Her "lists" would be longer than he could handle. He would get up when he thought the task was completed. Blake has never had any other "discipline" issues since 1st grade!

It was recommended Blake be classified and the reading program should be continued through 2nd grade. The Resource Room program was recommended for 3rd grade in place of a "normal" language arts class.

Lastly, I was told by the school psychologist, that Blake had so refined his coping skills, at such a young age, that he would have easily made it to 7th or 8th grade, before anyone knew he wasn't reading!!

I also made an appointment with a pediatric neurologist. He was very adamant that Blake was not ADD/ADHD and medication should not even be considered.

THIRD GRADE

Again the principal and I hand picked his teacher, Ms. Farley. Blake loved Ms. Farley! She was energetic, animated, young, creative, and enthusiastic with a great big smile. This definitely worked to her advantage. Blake couldn't wait to go to school each day to "help out" or to see what funny things they would do.

Socially, Blake was happy. He had both boys and girls as friends. He was excelling in sports and was an all around great kid. He continued to shine in Math while still struggling in Reading and Writing.

Blake still could not sound out words. He would add in letters that weren't even there. He was still writing from the bottom up and still reversing letters (b and d for example). I was told not to worry about that so much because they were soon going to learn script.

I went out and spent $200 on the "Hooked on Phonics" program. After watching the 1st tape, I had another revelation. Blake was not pronouncing his sounds correctly! The tapes show you how to shape your lips and he was not doing that for many of the letters. For example, the short i and short e sounds are very similar. I spoke to the Resource teacher and she tried to work with him.

They learned script and Blake's script was beautiful. I was told this was common because of the constant flow of the letters.

He seemed bored in Resource. He really hated to read unless someone was reading to him. He would complain that they worked too slowly.

I would ask the following questions, but never seemed to get answers that made sense:

1: Why does he do well on his spelling tests, but doesn't recognize some of the words a week or two later?

2: Why can he read this word today, but if you put it on a different page, it seems like he has never seen the word before? Or a different color page, a busy page, a different font...

3: Why can he do all this math stuff in his head (tax on a restaurant check), but on paper he has trouble writing out his steps?

4: Why when I study verbally with him, he often knows the answers, but an hour later for a test, it is like he has never heard of the material?

5: Why wasn't anyone else concerned about his handwriting?

6: Why was he still having trouble with some of the basic phonic sounds?

7: How could he have a "short-term" memory problem, but still be able to play Concentration and Chess?

8: Why weren't any of the implemented school programs really helping him?

FOURTH GRADE

Fourth grade is a big year in our elementary school because the students change classes for all their subjects. Blake had the good fortune of having a few teachers that were willing to go the distance and help in whatever way they could. The problem was no one seemed to know what would work.

He was excelling in Math and got the highest score one could get on the NYS 4th grade Math assessment! He loved math! This was in great part due to Mrs. Rose. Blake still talks about what a great teacher she was. Her sense of humor and her encouragement made such an impression on him.

He did okay in Science and Social Studies especially when he was able to use the computer or work on projects. Written tests were taken in the Resource Room and he had the questions read to him in a group setting. I believe there were about eight to ten students taking the test at the same time. There was no consistency in his grades.

Blake hated Resource! He constantly complained that he was bored and they made them do "stupid stuff". When I would speak to the teacher, everything she said seemed to be right, but I still did not see any significant progress. I was convinced Blake was brighter than most of the kids in Resource and that he already figured out how to play the game. He would give the teacher what she wanted so she would think he was "progressing nicely"! Resource was once again recommended for 5th grade. It seemed like that was our only alternative since nothing else was being offered.

At this point, Blake was now excelling in basketball and was also one of the few 10 year-olds pulled up to play in the Majors for Little League Baseball. He was also one of the popular boys in the class, and though he had many friends, he had the same two "best friends" since 1st grade.

FIFTH GRADE

Yea! Blake has Mr. Frank for homeroom and Science. Both my girls had him and he is probably one of the best teachers they will ever have in their educational careers. He single-handedly was and is one of the best things that happened to Blake in 5th grade. Blake loved Science.

Whatever Mr. Frank was teaching, Blake would just get it! He couldn't wait to get to homeroom and then go back again for Science. He wanted to do projects and help in class before school, during lunch, after school, whenever Mr. Frank was around. They (and other kids too) would talk school, sports, Spiderman, The Three Stooges and anything else the kids would bring up.

Unfortunately, I can't say the same for Math, Social Studies, and Resource.

Math was a nightmare. His teacher, though a nice guy, had no personality in the classroom. He was monotone, no expression and not clear in his explanations. Just the year before, he was teaching 3rd grade. He had a hard time making the transition and the kids suffered. Blake went from getting "A's" in 4th grade and doing so well on the State exam, to getting "C's".

Blake liked his Social Studies teacher but it was a lot of reading and writing of DBQs (data based questions). They did a lot of this in 4th grade too. Mrs. Kofe was great and she really tried to help Blake break the pieces down. Often there were articles he couldn't read on his own for several reasons: vocabulary was too difficult, it was written in script, the copies were not clear, it was too difficult for him to follow, just to name a few. Mrs. Kofe was very patient with him and she was always positive and upbeat, but he would just get so frustrated. It was my understanding they would work on the DBQs and other curriculum during Resource…

One of the tasks through the year was to learn all the state capitals. This was a trying task for Blake (and for Me!) of pure memorization. We tried to make a game out of it and make fun of all the names. We were very creative and for the most part he made it through. I don't know how many of them he would still remember today.

Since 3rd grade, on most days, I would have to sit with Blake while he completed his homework. I had gotten to the point I just couldn't do it anymore. If I couldn't sit with him because of a variety of reasons, it was becoming my fault he wasn't doing his homework. I think I did more homework in those two years than I did in my four years of high school. I went to speak to the Principal and she recommended Blake join their Homework Club. He could stay after school and do his work. There would be a teacher in the room to help any of the students that needed it. He did this for the remainder of the year, even though he fought me on it. Unfortunately his grades continued to drop.

Lastly, we have Resource. I found myself asking all the previously asked questions. There were still no concrete answers and still no significant progress. Blake could barely write or read script anymore because the teachers didn't make them use it. He was complaining more and more about reading yet still loved when I read to him. This was not nearly as often as I probably should have. I kept saying, It seems as if he needs to go back to 2nd grade for his handwriting and his phonics. He still kept complaining he was bored! He was getting a "B" in "English, but I am not sure compared to what.

Finally, halfway through the year, I made a decision to pull him out of Resource and place him the "regular" English class with Mr. Frank. The Principal, the School Psychologist, and the Resource Room teacher were all against this. I did it any way. Blake was excited to be with Mr. Frank. Blake's overall grade of B went down to a C. However, his spelling grades were about the same. More importantly, for the first time ever, Blake was excited about reading a book! Mr. Frank made the book come alive. Blake and I read the book together. Mr. Frank was pleased when he was telling me about how involved Blake would become in the book discussions. I am sorry I didn't have him in Mr. Frank's English class from the beginning of the year.

Another thing they did in Mr. Frank's class were these lateral thinking puzzles. You could only ask yes or no questions to figure out the "brain teasers". Blake loved these books and in fact, had me go out and buy more of them. He badly wanted to be able to "stump" his teacher!

His teachers, Principal, psychologist and I now needed to discuss what his 6th grade Middle School schedule would be. Blake was given another round of testing. It had been three years since he was first evaluated. Basically, we were told Blake's issues were unchanged since his last assessment.

It was decided his classes for the 6th grade would be: Science 6, Social Studies 6, Self-Contained Language Arts (I was unsure about this), Math 6 Enriched (at my insistence), Study Lab, and Band. He would also be taking art, health, computers, home & careers, and gym.

4

MIDDLE SCHOOL:
A FRESH START, NOT!
(6TH GRADE – 11 YEARS 2 MONTHS OLD)

"It was the best of times, it was the worst of times..."

(A Tale of Two Cities)

Blake was eager to be in the middle school. The week before school began, we walked around the building to find his classes. He wanted to make sure he knew where everything was. We met the Guidance Counselor (GC), Assistant Principal (AP) and the Principal.

The middle school is very large with over 2000 students.

On day one, Blake was up early and excited to take the bus for the very first time. We were "walkers" to the elementary school. He would finally be on the bus with one of his best friends, who is a year older.

First quarter went relatively well. I was in constant contact with his IEP (Individual Education Plan) teacher, Mrs. Karol. He was doing most of the homework on his own. In truth, they had very little of it. Blake was getting ready in the morning with little prodding from me. He was taking his tests in the testing center. Everything seemed to be taking a positive turn.

Second quarter was not as good. However, Blake seemed to be holding his own. Occasionally, he would miss a homework assignment. I was trying to remove myself from the homework equation. Blake's grades dropped a bit. Most of his teachers would tell me what a great kid he is, that he always participates in the discussions and often has a unique view on things!

Since **Math** was one of Blake's strengths, he was placed in **Enriched Math**. He was struggling and was only getting a C+. His teacher thought it would be best if he dropped down to "regular" math. She said if she "could work with him one on one, he could definitely stay in the enriched math but she does not have the time to do that." She also said she believed that "due to his learning disability, basically his processing issues, that it was as if he kept running into a wall." She felt he was getting frustrated. Then she told me, if he were in "regular" math, he would most probably be getting A's.

Blake dropped to "regular" math and ended up with only a B. He had been working with a tutor for several weeks before the final and they reviewed everything. He was in excellent shape for that final. He barely passed the exam.

Blake has always had a tendency to ask a lot of questions. You would think this would be a good thing especially in a **Science** class. From the beginning, the teacher did not seem to be a good match. This teacher told Blake, often, to "stop asking so many questions!" Also, the teacher told his students if they were late for any reason they would get detention.

At some point toward the end of Second Quarter (2Q), when Blake was not doing so well in Math, we found out he was rushing through his math test, at the testing center, so he would not be late for Science! Though on one level, Blake did know he was allowed extra time for his tests, his Science teacher said "lateness was not acceptable for any reason" and Blake never questioned it.

Blake dropped down to a D- for Third Quarter (3Q) in Math. I never got a note or phone call from this teacher and the progress report was not specific enough.

Blake also had a tutor for Science, for several weeks, before the final. The tutor was amazed at the amount of material Blake could not recall. It was as if he was seeing it for the first time. He passed his final with a

67 and went from a D- to a D+. Blake felt he knew so much more than these grades implied.

He liked his **Social Studies** teacher. They did several projects that went well. However, by 3Q he dropped to a D+. He got a Zero on his notebook quiz, basically because he didn't have much of a notebook!

I thought his IEP teacher was supposed to be helping him with his organizational skills. The notes in his Science and Social Studies notebooks were filled with "creative spelling". Blake could not possibly read what he wrote. I showed all of this to the Principal.

Let me go back a few months…In January, right after winter break, I had a meeting with his IEP teacher. I wanted to explain Blake's modus operandi (MO) regarding school. First grade was a lost year. For 2nd, 3rd & 4th grade, shortly after February break, he would begin to shut down. He would become bored and lose interest in the school routine. In 5th grade, this did not happen until after April break, totally because of Mr. Frank, a terrific and engaging teacher.

I wanted to let them know this so they would recognize the signs and be able to "head it off at the pass". The IEP teacher was supposed to impart this information to Blake's other teachers. I also had subsequent discussions with them as well.

As predicted, a few weeks after February break, I started to get THE phone calls. Blake was not handing in his homework, he is not completing his work, he appears to be daydreaming and so on and so on.

I then found out some of his teachers let the students pick their seats for 3Q. Blake was sitting in the back and usually surrounded by girls. I requested in the beginning of the year, that he always sit in the front and away from the door! This would be less of a distraction. Blake is extremely social with his peers and adults too. His ability to converse with anyone is amazing.

Blake was told he should be taking **Study Lab**. This class was useless. It was my belief this is where students were helped with their projects, homework, and organizational skills. He constantly complained about having to go. He said he would rather have a study hall where he could work on his own. Before entering 6th grade, Study Lab was suggested so I no longer had to be the "bad guy" when it came to homework and studying. There was very little support and guidance and it seemed to be a complete waste of time.

Because of Blake's Learning Disability, he was assigned to Self-Contained English. I would place this in the same category as the Resource Room in Elementary school. I believe his progress was minimal at best. Again, I believe he was bright enough to "play the game" so he would receive a "progressing nicely" on his progress report. He is supposed to be "meeting his goals" but I believe these goals are inferior.

One bright spot was that Blake was thrilled to be reading <u>Hatchet</u> in class. There was no outside reading required and I often asked why not? The response was that the students probably would not do it anyway!

His "progress" did not seem to be carrying over to his other subjects. I have the same questions as before. We do not seem closer to finding answers that make any sense.

At the beginning of Fourth Quarter (4Q), I met with Mrs. Base (Principal) because, at this point, I was out of my mind. Here was this kid everyone loved, everyone said how bright he was, but he was not passing 6th grade. I know everyone was trying to help (except his Science teacher) but nothing seemed to be working. Did someone drop the ball? Were we all at fault? Was Blake really not applying himself? Why did he just fall through the cracks? What were we missing?

While I do believe some of the responsibility should fall on my son's shoulders, I don't believe we have given him the skills necessary to take full responsibility. His grades improved somewhat during 4Q because I once again, became the "bad guy". At the same time, I hired a tutor to help with the review.

<u>MY OBSERVATIONS IN NO PARTICULAR ORDER:</u>
<u>END OF 6TH GRADE</u>

1: Blake does not write in script and I don't think he could read it with any confidence.

2: He still writes his letters and numbers from the bottom up and some are backwards.

3: He spells very creatively.

4: When he reads, he adds words and letters that are not there and misses words and letters that are there.

5: Blake does not like to read unless he is reading with me. I am the one reading and he is following along.

6: Sometimes he knows things, but does not know how or why he knows them.

7: He is social, athletic, has a great sense of humor, and a wonderful gift of gab.

8: Blake likes Chess, Uno, Game Cube, and Instant Messaging (IM) his friends.

9: He types very fast.

10: For the most part, he does not know the alphabet in order unless he sings the entire ABC song. (Which comes first R or G?)

11: Blake has learned to make up his own associations so he can remember things. Sometimes they work…

12: He plays drums in school.

13: He works with ease on the computer as well as anything electronic. He usually does this without looking at directions. He just seems to know.

14: Blake is always a "pleasure to have in class".

BLAKE'S OWN OBSERVATIONS:

It occurred to me through this whole process called school; no one had ever sat down and had a conversation with him. He was tested and then some things were put in place.

Sometimes he refers to himself as being "Sped" meaning stupid (short for Special Ed). I have often said I think he is so smart that he knows when to *act* stupid! I told Blake last week, I thought he was too smart to be getting "D's" in class. His reaction was one of exasperation. ***"Thank you. I have been trying to tell you that. They (teachers) just don't get it. They don't understand. No one will listen to me."***

I asked him what he thought would help. Trying to be funny (that is what he does to alleviate the tension), he asked if homework could be stopped. I told him I was sure that couldn't happen; so, let's move on. He then continued with the following and I am writing this just as he told it to me.

1: *"I don't understand what they mean a lot of times. I mean I know the words but they don't make sense together. Like in Math, we had to cut the triangle in half. What does that mean: from the point, across the middle? The teachers don't say what they mean. They should draw stuff on the board, then I would get it."*

2: *"They tell me to answer the questions on a page. When I go to hand in the homework, I don't know the answers and then I get in trouble. Then they tell me I had to read the pages before. Why didn't they tell me that to begin with?"*

3: *"Sometimes I just know the answers. I do it in my head. They always tell me to write everything down but I don't know what to write. When I try to write stuff down they tell me I am skipping steps. Then I get confused because I don't know what steps they are talking about. I didn't get the answer by doing "steps". I just knew it."*

MY REACTION:

In my heart and in my gut, I know Blake is extremely smart. I don't mean genius smart but his sense of logic and reasoning are definitely beyond those of his peers. I truly believe he belongs in several honors classes but needs to be taught "differently" than your typical student (if there is such a thing). He had great success with some teachers and no success with others. What is it that these teachers are doing and how do we get that for him on a consistent basis? We know what has been suggested in the past, has not been working. Where do we go from here?

Why is it that some services are offered to some students, but not to others, when their problems are similar? I recently found out that one boy was being given class notes from the teachers because he was having problems taking his own notes. Remember his Science and Social Studies notebooks? This service was never previously offered to him.

I also recently found out another boy was given his books on tape because he was having trouble reading the material. Again this was something that was never previously offered. I don't understand why. I was the one that had to ask for these services.

THE 6TH GRADE WRAP-UP

The reasons for my frustration should be obvious to anyone reading this. I am also greatly upset for my son and for the frustration he must be feeling. Is it any wonder he is starting to dislike school? Is it any wonder he is showing a defeatist attitude?

I have been following the district's suggestions for the past five years. We should not be dealing with some of these issues anymore, but they are not going away. What we thought would work, isn't. I have started to do my own research but I am not the "professional". I am now asking for the district's professionals to think outside the box and devise a plan of action that will enable Blake to improve his reading/comprehension level, elevate his self-esteem, and put him on the honors track where he belongs.

5

A Breakthrough!…Sort of…
(Summer Between 6th and 7th Grade)

Blake was not happy with his final grades in 6th grade. He was frustrated and I was exasperated. Through the summer, Blake was already becoming anxious about starting 7th grade. I made him a promise I would try to find out why he is having so much trouble in school.

It had been four years since Blake had been classified as Learning Disabled. I was now convinced, more than ever; we were missing a major piece to the puzzle. The so-called "experts" did not have any more of a clue than I did. It felt like Blake had become a guinea pig for their trial and error methods.

Now, I consider myself to be somewhat intelligent. However, it occurred to me I had never actually read the written part of Blake's 2nd and 5th grade psychological evaluations. After Blake had been tested, both times, my husband and I sat down and met with the school psychologist. For at least 1½ - 2 hours, she explained the results of the tests. Why would I have ever thought the written part would be different than the verbal explanation? How wrong I was…

It was a beautiful summer day in July. School had been out for about two weeks. I made myself a cup of iced coffee, gathered Blake's "papers", and proceeded to sit outside on my front porch, to read. I made my son a promise and I was determined to find some answers.

I began to read the 2nd grade evaluation. Within minutes, yes, minutes, my heart started racing. I broke out into a sweat. The wave of emotion was so strong and unexpected. I did not know if I should scream or cry. I did both. There was this one phrase that jumped off the page. Words I had never heard before as it related to Blake. Words, that in four years could possibly have answered some questions.

Anger was the next emotion to kick in and did so in a big way. All of a sudden, everything seemed to make sense.

What do I do with this information? My faith and trust in the "system" was now unbelievably broken. Was this neglect or just plain incompetence? The questions were flowing fast and furious. What started, I thought, as a simple reading activity, was now turning into my own personal research project.

I needed answers and explanations. I needed to go back to square one. I needed to see what worked for Blake and what didn't. I needed to question everything we had been told and re-evaluate the label of "Learning Disabled".

That little phrase read, **"...underscores dyslexic issues"**.

I spent the next few weeks talking to professionals around the country. One of my biggest resources was the International Dyslexia Association in New York City. It was suggested I read as much as I could. Two books in particular kept being recommended: <u>The Gift of Dyslexia</u> by Ronald D. Davis and <u>Upside-Down Brilliance</u> by Linda Kreger Silverman, Ph.D.

For the month of August, I might as well have gone back to school. I read, highlighted, took notes, made copies, spent hours in the library, talked to "specialists", pulled all nighters, couldn't sleep, and then started all over again.

Here is one of the ironic parts to this story. I received my BA in Sociology with a minor in Psychology and then went on for my Master's. My degree is in Counseling. The paradox is that we had the option of specializing in School Counseling or Special Education. You guessed it. I wanted nothing to do with Spec Ed and I took the School Counseling route. If I had only known then what I know now!

Once I understood what Dyslexia was, the next call I made was to Mr. Fuchs, the Director of Special Education for the school district. The next available date he had to meet with me was Blake's first day of 7th grade. I brought in all my information. I had questions. I was trying to use the "Can you help me?" approach. These games are so stupid. His solution was to give Blake an Alpha Smart word processor and a Pocket Speller that also pronounced words.

I took the "assistive technology" and went home completely frustrated. Blake never used either. I will briefly explain what these are, for those that don't know. The Alpha Smart looks like a laptop. It has a full keyboard and can do a lot of things. The major problem with it is the screen. You can only see a few lines at a time. This is a great piece of equipment for a student in elementary school. Not for a student who is quite accomplished on a computer.

There are two funny stories I have to insert here.

#1 - When Blake was in middle school, one of the courses offered (though he had no room in his schedule) was keyboarding. Blake adamantly refused to even think about taking the class. When I finally pushed him for a reason, he told me he did not want to learn how to play the piano!

#2 - Shortly after I had met with Mr. Fuchs, we were going to have a CSE (Committee on Special Education) meeting. I explained to Blake the district was adding a modification to his IEP (Individual Education Plan). He would now be able to use a word processor. Blake had no idea what that was. I explained it was the same as the computer. He had never heard the term "word processor" before.

The Pocket Speller was good in theory, but was not practical for Blake. First, the voice that says the words, out loud, was distorted. So you can imagine how confusing the sounds were for him. The spelling part was also confusing. You either already had to know how to spell something or pick from a list of words that may have been close. Neither was a good option for him.

Blake started 7th grade excited that this year will be much better.

6

GETTING THROUGH MIDDLE SCHOOL

7TH GRADE

Blake began 7th grade with high hopes, as did I. After all, I was sure what his issues were and more importantly what they weren't. I was going to contact the teachers, re-evaluate his Individual Education Plan (IEP) and start anew.

The "honeymoon" lasted about a month. We were still dealing with several questions related to the IEP:

1: Which special ed teacher will be responsible?

2: How will his progress be measured? Use of observation by itself is not measurable.

3: Checklists were hardly ever used and when I asked to see them, they were never produced.

4: One of the paragraphs, on the IEP, reads, "Reading vocabulary words at his instructional grade level with 70% mastery." If Blake had completed these goals with "70% mastery" in the earlier grades, we would not be having these same issues year after year.

Bottom line is, his GOALS are not measurable. There is still no accountability on the district's part when these so called goals are not met.

Five months later, Blake's goals have not been changed and are still not measurable.

Blake was placed in a **self-contained English class**. This is the class for students who are either slow or need more than the traditional support of a "regular" teacher. I knew he did not belong there, but I was not offered any other options. It was a nightmare! Most of the kids in this class had behavior problems and were very disruptive. The teacher seemed ill equipped to handle them because she wanted to be their "friend". At one point, she even asked the boys if "her butt looked big" in her jeans! I have documentation of work not graded properly and papers that just don't make sense. The teacher was very disorganized and Blake was quickly melting down.

Again, I went in complaining and now we had to change his entire schedule. Blake was not happy with me even though he did want to get out of that class. I always seemed to end up being the bad guy.

Due to scheduling issues, Blake could not have study lab every day, so it was suggested that he come in BEFORE SCHOOL for **additional Study Lab** time, which he did. Every other morning, Blake had what was called a Zero period. This made for a very long day.

He had been playing trumpet since 4th grade and continued playing through 6th grade. In 5th grade, he also started taking drum lessons. Blake decided to switch to the drums for the 7th grade **Band**. He started in the Cadet Band (lower level). Halfway through the year, the students are able to try out for Concert Band, which Blake did. *Blake was told he did not make Concert Band because he could not sight read.*

Who knew that sight-reading was a pre-requisite? If we had known, I would have said something. Should a student be penalized from trying out for the higher-level band because they have reading issues? Out of frustration, Blake dropped band. The drums and trumpet have not been picked up since.

Unfortunately, there are a good number of students who are "dumped" into **ASL (American Sign Language)** because, it is thought, they can't handle one of the other languages offered. This was not so in Blake's case. Both his sisters sign, as do his cousins. Blake wanted to take ASL. The teacher, Ms. Sunny, was very nice, but had absolutely no idea what she was getting herself into. There were many discipline problems in this class as well and she was getting very overwhelmed. Blake did well the beginning of the school year, but as the teacher became more and more frustrated, Blake's grades went down dramatically.

His A- went down to a D+, and then averaged out to a B-. He also ended up with an 87 on his final after getting a D+ for 4Q. In ASL, it really is not possible to get an 87 on the final, if you don't know the work.

Math has never really been a problem for Blake. In fact, he was recommended for Honors Math.

He did well in **Science** but **FAILED** his final with a 55. This was another one of his teachers that did not get tenure.

Blake really liked his **Social Studies** class. The teacher was very demonstrative and artistic. However, he **FAILED** the final with a 52.

Blake **FAILED Home and Careers** with an F! He did not want to take this class and I found out later he did not have to. He liked the cooking part but if he did not participate in the other "tasks", the teacher would not let them cook. Hence the F.

This was a wasted class where Blake could have been getting more instructional/reading help instead of going in for a Zero period!

Report card issues: An entire chapter will be devoted to this issue - **Be Afraid.**

8TH GRADE: MURPHY'S LAW

Blake was due to be re-evaluated. The testing began and took four days, over a six-week period. My first issue was that it had taken so long to complete. When I finally received Blake's psych-ed report, I knew right away there were errors. Initially, the main inaccuracy was in the Psychologist's observation. I knew, for a fact, she had observed Blake in a different period that was stated. After several phone calls and emails, as well as a phone call to Dr. Miller (head of Psych), Ms.

Heart (psychologist) admitted to me, in a hand written note, that she had **"made an error when she was cutting and pasting"**.

I continued to express my concern about the results themselves. I kept comparing previous IEPs, but was obviously too close to the situation. However, I kept expressing my unease to anyone who would listen (Head of Psych, Psych, Principal, and more). They told me that everything was correct.

In January, I decided to have another Special Ed teacher look at the results and she noticed **the Decoding piece of the testing was not done!** I reported this back to the district and *no one* seemed to think *that this was a problem.*

I continued to complain that the Goals were not measurable.

About this time, I made an appointment with Ms. Rice (Head of HS Spec Ed) to talk about Blake entering the High School. After being in the district for so long, I knew it could take months to get anything accomplished. I did not want to wait until the end of the school year.

Our meeting was counter-productive. After looking at Blake's testing and telling her I thought the results were incorrect, Ms. Rice said, "Your son is clearly not dyslexic." I told her she did not have enough information to make that kind of statement.

Blake began 8th grade in a **self-contained English** class and was moved to a **Regular** class 2nd Quarter. Mrs. Bear used a lot of positive reinforcement techniques that seemed to work well with him. However, he **FAILED** his final with a 61.

Finally a Study Lab class that was effective! Mr. Carlos was wonderful. He did everything right. He followed up with the teachers. He reported back to me in a timely fashion. He kept Blake focused, organized, interested and excited about most of his classes.

Ms. Sunny did not return to teach ASL. The year started with Ms. Hirsch (she pops back up again in 10th grade!). Since it was basically the same kids as last year, behavior was still a major problem in the classroom. Blake managed to hold on, but we had problems with her, regarding record keeping and test scores. I kept these emails in my file.

We then find out Ms. Hirsch is going out on maternity leave. The leave replacement teacher is Ms. Bennie, and she is great. She had no problem controlling the class. The kids liked her and they even learned! Blake's grades went from a C+ for 2Q to an A- for 3Q. Unfortunately, Ms. Hirsch returned three-quarters of the way through 4Q. All the issues in class started all over again. The kids were miserable.

Even though Blake was recommended for **Honors Math**, I was strongly advised, at the last committee meeting, not to place him there. We were simultaneously moving him into a **Regular English** class as well. "They" thought it would be too difficult for him to be in both. I should let him stay in the **Regular Math** so he can do well. I took their advice. *In hindsight, this was a huge mistake, on my part!*

Fortunately **Science,** this year, was not a problem.

Social Studies was a disaster almost from Day One. Blake could not follow what the teacher was talking about. His tests never seem to cover what they learned in class. Mr. Eddy yelled a lot. Blake never reacts well to yelling, especially when he did not do anything wrong. He struggled immensely (D+/1Q, F/2Q). He improved a bit 3Q, but by 4Q, he just couldn't take the class anymore. Everything he did was wrong. Blake **FAILED** his final with a 51 and ended up with a D for the year.

In 8th grade, the students take a **Tech** class. Blake **FAILED** Tech with an F! We are still not sure how because he made his clock (which came out great) and finished his car. No one ever answered my emails. I did not press this because I knew the grade was not important. I was learning to pick and choose my battles.

Also in 8th grade, in New York State, the students need to take what is called the ELA (English/Language Arts) State Test. The purpose of this is to test for state standards. It is suppose to help flag students that are falling behind. I don't know of a single student who was truly behind that the teachers did not know about beforehand.

Blake reported to the assigned room for his ELA. When he got there, his name was not on the list. The teacher sent him down to the office. It took about a half hour with the Assistant Principal to find a room for him. He started the test about 45 minutes late. By that time, he was in no state of mind to take a test. He was frustrated and aggravated which is certainly understandable, under the circumstances. More on state tests later...

The Testing Center is supposed to be a place where certain students can take their exams using their modifications. There was never any consistency here. Often, they were just staffed with TAs (Teaching Assistants - sometimes just a parent working as a TA), not trained teachers who could work with special needs students.

One major example of this is a day Blake went to school early to take a math exam. The test instructions said to put the answer in simplest form. When he finished, the TA said his answers were not in simplest form. Blake said it was okay that he leaves it that way. An argument ensued. Blake was so frustrated he walked out of the room and down to the Guidance office. He did not want to say something he shouldn't. The TA wrote him up as being insubordinate! The end result was that Blake was correct. This TA could have handled the situation in any number of ways but chose not to. After all, who was the adult in the room? Why are you starting an argument with him? This had a major impact on Blake and it took almost two years before he would use the testing center in high school.

7

HIGH SCHOOL: A NEW BEGINNING

9TH GRADE (2006-2007)

Blake was excited to be starting High School. This was a new beginning. A new school, new people, new opportunities, what could be bad?

As we soon found out, it was the same old "stuff", just dressed up differently.

Unfortunately, Blake's 2006-2007 IEP was based on **incomplete testing in 8th grade**. All his goals, except for one, were still not measurable. There was no accounting for his reading disability. **They never did the decoding piece of the testing.**

On 3/4/07, I sent a letter to Mr. Fuchs, saying I felt the newest IEP, based on the 2/12/07 meeting, was still inadequate for a variety of reasons. Mr. Fuchs received this letter on 3/6/07. A copy of it is in Blake's binder.

IEP Progress Report 5/2/2007: The Progress Report states at what percent success Blake should accomplish these goals but it does not say at what percent he is progressing. Some of these are one-shot deals such as the Career and Vocational Activities. The "Procedures to Evaluate Goals" are vague at best.

Blake was struggling in **Intensive English** primarily due to the vocabulary tests. His teacher, Ms. Sinto, was very concerned and tried to be helpful. Blake made a comment that he knew what the words meant, but when he took a test, he did not understand the choices given to him. When I questioned his teacher, she said Blake was correct. The choices

31

they give them on the exams may not be the ones they studied. She explained to me (and others in the school have repeated the same)that "they expect the students to come in with a certain level of vocabulary." I have been questioning this "wisdom" ever since. Supposedly, the students are to acquire this additional vocabulary from their outside reading.

My argument was this:

1: Blake has been in self-contained classes so his reading level would not be the same as others.

2: If Blake were dyslexic, and at the time I believe this was probably the case, he would have trouble picking up additional vocabulary from the outside reading. The doctor who tested him later confirmed this belief.

3: Even the College Board gives students the top 200 words they should know before they take the SATs. The choices match what is given to them.

There was an additional problem with the English midterm. There was, at least one word, on the midterm, the students had never seen before on any list or in any book, they had read for school. There may have been more but one word stood out the most. The students had to pick the word closest in meaning. **(Zenith - choices are 1: moon, 2: stars, 3: journey, 4: acme).** They were to use deductive reasoning. Blake did use his deductive reasoning but got the wrong answer. "Acme" is the answer. Most adults I asked did not know what it meant. When you say the word, two responses came up most often: a grocery chain and the mail order company from the Road Runner!

Blake ended up with a D+ for the mid-semester average and **FAILED his midterm with a 56.**

The only suggestion I was offered was to move Blake to a **Self-contained English** class where he ended the year with a B.

Ms. Sinto temporarily left the school for personal reasons shortly thereafter.

Blake was placed in **Study Lab**. This class was supposed to be helpful in giving him support. It was where they would work on the goals and objectives (G & O) listed on his IEP.

First semester, he was with Ms. Salve. Blake liked her, but I found her to be ineffective. I have an email from her stating that after five months into the school year, *she would like to start working on Blake's G & O*. There were several Bio projects that were worked on in Study Lab. I did not feel they were monitored properly.

This could have been an excellent time to work on strategies to self-correct or self-monitor. In addition, she was also a Science teacher, which we thought would be helpful since Blake was struggling in Science. This turned out not to be the case. According to Mr. Jack (Assistant Principal), she was very inexperienced.

Second semester, he had Ms. Davey and Mr. Schack. This combination worked out much better, in part, because Blake was moved into Mr. Schack's **Self-contained Global**.

Blake did really well in **American Sign Language (ASL)** with Ms. Tell. Unfortunately, the behavior issues, previously in the middle school, carried over to the high school. In fact, at one point an assistant was brought into the class. He was not truly an assistant but rather a *Security Guard*! Blake's final grade was an A-. *Ms. Tell was so overwhelmed; she did not return to teach and sought out a grad program instead.*

Blake's best subject was always math, until this year. For 9th grade, he was placed in **Math Year 1, Math A**. Ms. Creek was very nice, but her "rules" were too strict. For example, the students were not allowed to turn their homework in late. In the beginning, Blake, due to documented organizational issues, would leave his homework in his locker. He would get a Zero. She also graded the homework from Zero - 2 pts. Blake would do his homework. Maybe he would not show all his work or not do the examples her way or leave some problems out because he didn't know how to do them. He would get a Zero or a One. In my opinion, homework should not be graded. It should be checked to see if it is done and then gone over. Blake was very frustrated with the homework situation.

In the beginning, many of the worksheets were handwritten. It took several weeks to realize that Blake could not read her handwriting. We were finally able to get them printed out.

On the midterm exam, there was a word problem where Blake mixed up the names Maura and Mary. I explained that this is not testing him on the material, but rather his reading and listening skills. Why couldn't it have been changed to Ken and Mary? I was told it would change the test. The person's name had no bearing on the example. I voiced my disapproval.

Blake did go to extra help a few times, but was more frustrated than before. He **FAILED the midterm with a 63** but, with the help of his tutor, passed the final with an 86. He also ended up with an 84 on the NYS Regents exam, because of his tutor.

Regular Biology with Mrs. Mace did not begin well starting with the "contract" the first day. I found the contract to be very negative toward the students. It did not give a positive outlook for the year. I copied this to Blake's Guidance Counselor (Mrs. House) and Mrs. Rice (Sp. Ed.) with my comments.

On Wed, November 15, 2006 at 11am, I had a meeting with Mr. George (AP) and Mrs. Koch (Dept Chair) to discuss Biology. Mr. George said learning Bio was like learning a new language. Based on this discussion, Mr. George felt we should have an IST (Instructional Support Team) meeting. He was going to follow up on that. In the meantime, it was suggested we move Blake **out of Regular and into an Intensive class.**

Second quarter started with Mrs. Obie's **Intensive Bio** class. This began well with Mrs. Obie even sharing some of her experiences with another school district. She too has a son with "issues". Blake continued to have problems with certain projects: *some of which have never been resolved.* I had asked for these projects to be reviewed by an independent person. My requests have been unsatisfactorily answered. I believe Blake was graded improperly based on his IEP. He was not supposed to be penalized for spelling. Also some of the directions were not specific and there was no way to self-correct. I still have these projects, in case I could ever get them reviewed. He **FAILED his midterm with a 63** and ended the class with a C-. He managed a 71 on the regents. Again, I believe, it was due to his tutor.

I need to clarify and emphasize that all tutors for Blake were privately hired and paid for by us.

There were also major problems with the Bio Regents Review sessions. First, the notice came home with the wrong information. I have a copy of this. Second, when Blake went to the initial session, there were so many students crammed into the room, he had to sit half on the back counter and half in a sink! The other sessions were moved to a room to accommodate the 100-150 students that were showing up. I don't think there is anyone who has ever worked with Blake that would say this is a good learning environment for him. Yet he did go. The one time he left early, Mrs. Obie chastised him. There were many other documented issues with Mrs. Obie, but it would just be more of the same.

Blake liked Mr. Brace for **Global History 9**. Unfortunately, Blake had trouble grasping the reality of "Global History". No pun intended but it was foreign to him. He could not relate. He had trouble with the names, not only writing them but pronouncing them as well. Too many things sounded similar.

Even though Blake got a D for 8th grade Social Studies and a 51 on his final, no one recommended Blake for Intensive Global History 9. I did not even know it existed.

Blake ended up with a D+ for 1st semester and a 66 on his midterm. It was suggested we move Blake to **self-contained** since he lost most of the first half of the year.

Interesting note: *Even though Blake was doing terribly in Global, it was the only midterm that he passed! (Except for ASL.) I attribute this to* *the fact that another student gave the Self-contained level Study guide to Blake the night before the midterm.*

He was switched to **self-contained Global** with Mr. Schack. He did well with him. It also helped that Blake had him part time for **Study Lab**. He ended up with a B for a final grade. *Unfortunately, Mr. Schack was not hired back to the district.*

TV PRODUCTION 1: Blake did well in this and will probably pursue level 2. *Unfortunately, Ms. Fierce left the district.*

REPORT CARD ISSUES: The district policy is when a student changes levels; the original grades get dropped from the report card so the student can start anew with a clean slate. This particular year, it was not done for English, Global or Bio.

On the 4Q progress report, the only negative comments came from the Bio teacher. This is in contrast with her 3Q comments.

Blake started the **Wilson Reading Program** privately at our expense from March 12th - April 18th *(www.wilsonlanguage.com - the Wilson Reading System (WRS) is the flagship program of Wilson Language Training and the foundation of all other Wilson programs. Based on Orton-Gillingham principles, WRS is a highly-structured remedial program that directly teaches the structure of the language to students and adults who have been unable to learn with other teaching strategies, or who may require multisensory language instruction.)*

Unfortunately, Blake's Wilson tutor stopped for the summer. He completed books 1-3 out of 12.

There was a major issue with the **Math midterm**. Blake was told to go to one room and then was moved to another. We were told previously this would happen for English and Global but it was not specified for Math. When Blake tried to explain that this is where he was told to be, he was told it was being changed with no explanation: *so much for advocating for himself.*

On Monday, January 29, 2007, a woman Blake did not know called him out from Study lab. He was brought to the special Ed office where she tried to have a discussion with him about his "future". This was the first day back to school, after midterms and unfortunately, ***he had just found out that he failed most of them***. He was really not in any mood to discuss his future plans, especially with someone he did not know.

Blake came home that day and for the first time ever, I found him questioning his ability and saying, "Maybe I really am stupid"! His comments were: It was dumb, I am not going to BOCES, Why is she talking to me about this now, I don't even know her, and Who does she think she is? He was somewhat cooperative because it is not in his nature to be rude.

MEETINGS, MEETINGS AND MORE MEETINGS...

Wed 11/15/06 11am: mtg with Mr. George and Mrs. Koch re: Bio

Wed 11/29/06 8:30am: Instructional School Team (IST) mtg

Tues 12/5/06 10am: mtg with Mr. Jack - AP (2 ½ - 3 hrs)

Fri 1/19/07: Blake tested by Dr. X at NYC Hospital (8:30-4)

Mon 2/12/07 1:15pm: CSE (Committee on Special Education) mtg

Fri 2/16/07 10am: Final testing results mtg with Dr. X

Thurs 6/14/07 1pm: CSE mtg

Thurs 7/12/07: **Received phone call about Blake taking a Wilson summer program to begin the following Monday 7/16/07 (4 days later!)**

Tues 8/14/07 1pm: Mtg with Mrs. Lackey (Asst Superintendent of Pupil Personnel Services), Mr. Jack - AP, and Mr. Vick - Principal. This was the first time Mrs. Lackey had met Mr. Jack.

8

DECIDING TO TEST OUTSIDE THE DISTRICT

As Blake entered 7th grade, I wanted to have him tested outside the district. I truly felt they had failed him and did not give him the proper support he needed. I also felt that, if in fact Blake was dyslexic, they did not know how to work with him. I needed to know for sure, but did not trust what I was being told by the "experts" in the district.

The major obstacle to having Blake evaluated, at that time, believe or not, was my husband. The testing would have cost about $3000 and was not covered by insurance. He did not want to spend the money. He felt the district should be doing their job. I feel there was also a part of him that believed exactly what so many teachers had told us; that Blake was not paying attention, not focusing. He felt Blake should get his act together. We had several fights about this over the next few years.

In an earlier chapter, I express my anguish over Blake's 8th grade evaluation. They neglected to do the Decoding piece of the testing. I called Ms. Heart, the School Psychologist. She was very nice but also very inexperienced. I told her the written part of the report is wrong. She said she will "look into it". She did and told me everything is fine. The district school psychologist, Dr. Miller, was also looking into it. **Three weeks later, I get an email and an updated report.** Ms. Heart corrected her "cutting and pasting" errors, but they still insisted the numbers on the report were correct.

My husband's opinion was that the district should just retest him. At this point, I did not trust anything or anyone regarding the procedures.

For me, it was three strikes and you're out. We still continued to disagree for the next year.

Shortly into Blake's freshman year, I had enough. I did my research. I wanted him evaluated by the best in the field. I did not care whether or not they were "in the plan". I wanted to be sure the district could not argue with the results, if my intuition was correct. We ended up taking Blake to one of the top NYC Neuropsychological Centers. The Pediatric Director and her assistant were going to administer the test. It was a full day, a full neuropsychological evaluation. The testing cost $4000 and was not covered by insurance (That's another book!).

It was a three-step process. Step One was a meeting with me to get a family background (December of freshman year). There was also quite a bit of intake paperwork to complete. Step Two (January of freshman year) was the full test day with Blake. Step Three (February of freshman year) was the results meeting.

My husband did accompany me to meet Dr. X. It was also on my birthday. The first words out of the Doctor's mouth were, **"Blake could be a poster child for Developmental Dyslexia. He is in 9th grade, reading at approximately a 4th, maybe 5th, grade level!"**

I just started crying. I wanted to scream, punch and just lash out at everyone, including my husband. I knew something was wrong. Then came the guilt. I was so overwhelmed. I failed my son. Why didn't I do what I knew was right, years ago? Why did I listen to these people? Why was I so nice to them (at least most of the time)? I was upset. I knew my intuition was right yet I was happy to know I was not going crazy.

For years, I had been telling them something was wrong; telling them we had to think outside the box; telling them we were missing a piece to the puzzle. No one was listening. They would put on a band-aid and hope I would go away. When the band-aid fell off, I would be right back. The results were always the same. Blake never seemed to progress the way they said he would.

Guilt quickly turned into anger. I needed some additional outside help.

9

THE DECISION TO HIRE
A STUDENT ADVOCATE

This decision was easy. I was frustrated with everything. I did not know what else to do. I needed an outside opinion. I needed someone who could look at my son's history and give us advice on what to do next. I needed some support from someone "in the know".

I now knew what the problem was, but I did not know how to change or fix things. I no longer trusted anyone in the school to do what was in Blake's best interest. Where do I go? Who do I call?

In our town, there is a Volunteer Counseling Center. I called them just to see if, in fact, they handle situations in the school system. A very nice woman took some information and told me I would get a call back by the end of the day.

I felt like the Mom on the Huntington Learning Center commercial when they tell her "You made the right call." I just wanted to cry.

I got a phone call back and to my surprise they did handle school cases, sort of. Most often, it was for a student with behavior issues or those failing that did not have any parental support. The Counselor was, however, very informative and asked me for the history of the case. The next day she called again with all kinds of suggestions of how I should approach the district. What I should say, using the right terminology, and who to follow up with.

At least, for now, I felt I had a plan. The bantering with the school went on for months. It was the same game of run around.

In March of Blake's freshman year (one month after he was diagnosed), I attended the International Dyslexic Association Conference in NYC. It was there, during a session on Student Advocacy, I met Kay. She had twenty years experience in the field and had previously taught the subject matter. It was a good fit and about one month later, we hired her.

I wanted someone to go with me to the next IEP meeting to hear how I was being treated. More importantly, to also hear how Blake's issues were not being taken seriously.

Boy, did she get an earful!

41

10

CSE Meeting:
(Committee on Special Education)

June 14, 2007

This was just another of "way too many meetings". However, it was important because we now had an official diagnosis of Developmental Dyslexia. We also had a professional opinion that most of what the district had tried to do for Blake, over the past six years, was a waste of time. For the most part, the easy fix was to just drop him down a class level. The reality was Blake could have possibly been in some advanced classes with additional support. He was not slow.

The sad fact is that there were several classes in high school Blake wanted to take (Forensics and Statistics to name a few). He was told he couldn't because of a low grade in a somewhat related previous class. We have taught him to always try. If you don't try, you will never know if you could have done it, or even if you really liked it.

Several days before the meeting, I sent a detailed letter to the administration outlining my concerns:

June 5, 2007

Dear Ms. Rice, CSE Chair

With full confidence that each of the members of Blake's IEP team shares a common interest with us in providing him with an appropriate educational program in the least restrictive environment, we are outlining below priorities for guiding our discussion during our annual IEP meeting scheduled for June. Our intention in doing so is to come to the earliest possible resolution on the issues that confront us as a team. We have categorized the team's decision-making responsibilities into two areas. These are:

Highest priority (to be determined at the June IEP meeting):

1: With the goal of salvaging what we can from the current school year, we propose that the district conduct an objective review of SY 2006-2007 corrected assignments (homework projects/tests/quizzes in Biology and Math) to ascertain if IEP modifications were taken into consideration and consistently applied; and

2: Similarly, to build on the skills that Blake has developed in the reading program we initiated and paid for outside of school, we propose that the district take immediate fiscal responsibility for appropriate reading instruction (see evaluation conducted by Dr. X) to address his reading deficits including compensatory individually based summer reading instruction (given his age and the lack of appropriate services since 2nd grade).

Secondary priority (to be determined prior to September 1):

1: The development of an IEP with clearly defined and measurable goals addressing his areas of need with primary emphasis on continuation of intensive reading instruction which is systematic, phonologically-based, and individualized and includes high-order reading comprehension skills, as well as addressing spelling and writing skills (the comprehensive and high quality evaluation conducted by Dr. X elucidates findings of the district's evaluators and established clear need for these services). The IEP should also focus on his well-documented need for executive function skills training; and, it should address vocational planning as well as other needs identified by any additional evaluations;

2: The development of improved methods of communication

between school and home to be included on the IEP (under Report to Parents section) and consistently followed;

3: An assistive technology evaluation to be conducted by evaluators knowledgeable of reading/writing deficits and the acquisition and use of devices subsequently recommended including training for staff, parents and student in the use of these devices;

To date, we have addressed our concerns about Blake's inappropriate programming by initiating a significant number of formal and informal interactions with district staff at all levels, providing expert evaluative information to clarify Blake's present levels of performance in reading, and compensating for a lack of appropriate instructional programming by paying for trained tutors to teach him at home. Despite the IEP team's agreement, based on the district's own evaluative documentation, that Blake has demonstrated reading difficulties since second grade, the district has not provided appropriate interventions to address this acknowledged need or arranged for appropriate reading evaluations to be conducted. Even his current IEP, as a ninth grader, identifies his reading deficits but fails to include annual goals to address them. It is imperative that we begin to move forward in salvaging what we can of this school year, putting in place some programs this summer that will compensate for failure to provide them during previous school years, and, finally, laying the groundwork for the development of an appropriate IEP to begin the 2007-2008 school year. It is our hope that with focused planning on the development of an appropriate IEP, the district will be better able to keep its legal obligation to provide copies of the IEP to each of his teachers and staff working with Blake prior to the first day of school. This will better enable him to transition into the next school year on more solid footing than has been available during the current year.

Prior to our IEP meeting it is absolutely crucial that we have your assurance that Blake's testing accommodations will be fully implemented for his finals, which begin on June 13. I have enclosed with this letter a list of individual school staff who are known to Blake and who could read his tests to him as required by his IEP. <u>To counteract the confusion and lack of attention to his reading deficits this year it would be helpful if Blake could take his final exams in a room without other students being present.</u> To include Blake in the potential fading of these accommodations which we think may be possible in the future it would be advisable to have Blake attempt to read aloud each of his exams and to use the required reader only if necessary or they could alternate reading. In this way we could begin to prepare Blake for initiating the need for his accommodations when necessary. I would like your confirmation in writing to me no later than June 11 that one of these individuals has been scheduled to accommodate him for each of his final exams and I would ask you to identify the rooms where he will be taking each of his exams.

With this knowledge Blake can come to the exams with confidence that he will do well. The district's full implementation of these accommodations will serve as a message to Blake and to us that you are willing to comply with the provisions for implementation of the IEP as mandated by the Part 200 Regulations. By ending the school year in this way we can begin to move forward to appropriately address Blake's needs for special education services and programs and prepare him for some very positive long-term outcomes.

Recognizing that your time is valuable and that we, too, have busy schedules, we hope that our meeting with you will be focused on coming to a decision on each of the above issues. We look forward to working with you.

Sincerely, Elaine and Charles *[end of letter]*

I also had a full agenda of issues that I wanted addressed:

ITEMS TO BE DISCUSSED AT THE JUNE 14TH, 2007
BLAKE'S ANNUAL REVIEW/CSE MEETING

In no particular order:

1: An Indirect Consultant Teacher to:

    a: Review Blake's tests/quizzes/projects/assignments to check for specific directions, rubrics, follow-ups, clarifications

    b: To act as a Liaison between myself and his teachers

2: Have Blake tested one on one for large exams, midterms, finals, regents when deemed necessary by him, me and/or the teacher

3: Extra time - double

4: Directions read and reread

5: Specific directions

6: Tools to self-check and self correct

7: Gym - if graded next year??

8: Summer Reading Assignments

9: Reimbursement for testing and tutoring

10: Payment of future tutoring and remedial services

11: Math

    a: Review all homework given a 0 or 1 out of 2. If homework was handed in, it should get at least 1 point. There are many of these that Blake didn't "show all the work" or "didn't do it on a separate piece of paper". At least he did something and turned it in!

    b: Notebooks should not be checked for a grade unless it is going to help him. I have been complaining about this since 6th grade. Organization issues. Poor grades do not help him do it any better.

    c: Worksheets should be given with enough space to do the work so Blake does not have to transfer the equations.

    d: Possible use of calculator/computer to print out work.

    e: Blake gets a's, u's, p's and q's mixed up at times. He also gets the + and x, and b's and d's mixed up especially when he is writing out the work. *[end]*

By now, I had hired Kay as our student advocate because I felt I needed her help. Neither Kay nor I could have expected what was to happen next. I was never so happy that I thought to tape this meeting.

THE FOLLOWING IS KAY'S REVIEW OF THE MEETING:

{With full knowledge that critical members of the team had to leave the meeting in an hour and a half, the team spent at least 60 minutes rehashing old business and leaving about thirty minutes to discuss Blake's IEP for 2007-2008. This effectively threw [Mom] off track and was intended to be intimidating because it was not based on any factual information or rational review of the record or knowledge of Blake's needs. It was simply an attack on [Mom's] role as an interested and involved parent.

Included in the district diatribe were the following familiar nuggets: [Mom's] multiple e-mails to teachers who do not respond to direct questions or provide information that is vital to Blake doing well qualifies as "abusive" behavior on the part of [Mom] (something teachers' don't deserve but apparently parents do); allegations that Blake isn't trying/working hard enough or isn't motivated or engaged; assertion that SED is changing the rules for the way IEP's are written ("one IEP for all") and that these rules won't be available until July; and assertions that there are "far needier students" than Blake.

Summer plans for individualized reading instruction for Blake were pushed off to the Director of Pupil Personnel for a decision. None of the issues outlined in the letter sent to the team prior to the meeting was raised or resolved. As a result, [Mom] was not even made aware of what was in the IEP until the last five minutes of the meeting and then was expected to sign it without reading it. A request to see a copy of it was denied ("it is against policy to let parents have a copy") and only after persistent urging was [Mom] given a copy and then only of the last two pages containing the IEP goals. The evaluation results which led to the formation of the goals were not made available to her. There was a demand made that the IEP <u>had</u> to be signed by June 24 with no apparent connection at all to the need for [Mom] to see it in whole and to have time to read and ask questions about it. A school psychologist present at the meeting (but who had never met Blake and who sat silent throughout the meeting) finally agreed to print out the last two pages of the proposed IEP for [Mom]. The proposed goals were taken from a pre-packaged program (IEP Direct) and will be evaluated by "observation checklists" scheduled for the 4th marking period. It doesn't seem likely that one individual using "observation" as the only way of assessing the success of the intervention and only required to assess it at the end of the year is going to be successful for Blake. It is difficult to say why Blake's measurement of success is 75% for some goals and 8% for others. In one case (completing a level one vocational assessment) only 65% accuracy is required of Blake (life after school is of less concern, I suspect, to the district)!

The reading issue which is paramount to Blake's success was addressed by the following offerings: 1) a specialized school costing the district and Blake a great price (to be educated in a segregated setting with disabled peers and no contact with non-disabled peers would be a inappropriate and is an empty gesture, at best, because the district knows that there is no opening at a school for students with LD at this time of year); 2) prescriptive English class with ED students who are failing all of their subjects and receiving counseling 4X weekly and who have behavioral issues (Blake's needs are not consistent with these students' needs and it is a totally inappropriate setting for him/smacks of a punitive intent); 3) a self contained English class; 4) an intensive (smaller class size) English class. These are all versions of English classes.

NONE OF THESE OPTIONS ADDRESS READING ISSUES PER SE. Blake was offered an 8th period Wilson reading program three times a week in a group setting with two alternating periods of resource room (unstructured and primarily devoted to homework/minimum individualized instruction/clear documentation that this is not working this year to meet his needs). His comprehensive reading evaluation conducted by Dr. X indicates a clear and immediate need for individualized intensive instruction to begin now. <u>She recognizes that because of the district's delay in addressing Blake's needs earlier, there is a significant problem of engaging and motivating him.</u> THIS IS RELATED TO HIS DISABILITY AND IS NOT WILLFUL, AS THE CSE MEMBERS ASSERTED. Motivation and engagement are the challenges Blake's teachers now face.

Accommodations in all classes for Blake's reading/spelling/writing impairments have yet to be consistently implemented or applied. No one oversees the systematic implementation of these accommodations but each teacher "does his/her own thing" and most rely on Blake to initiate and insist on the accommodations. Recognizing and taking seriously this aspect of his disability (inability to ask for help or recognize when he needs it, organizational deficits including time management/getting accurate homework assignments and following through on them etc.) **are important responsibilities for his teachers to attend to.** NO CLEAR DETERMINATION WAS MADE ABOUT THIS ISSUE FOR 2007-2008 except that Blake's IEP goals appear to be no different from ANY STUDENT IN GENERAL EDUCATION: Blake needs to write down his homework assignments, bring (don't they mean "take"?) homework assignments home, accept assistance from teachers without protest, refocus when his attention is drifting. How do these simple statements qualify as IEP goals? How do we know if Blake is doing them without COMMUNICATION in place with the parents? What help is he getting to do them and how is that help being implemented? If only the special education teacher is required to implement these goals, how are expectations applied to ALL classes Blake takes? THESE STUDY SKILLS GOALS RAISE MORE QUESTIONS THAN THEY SHOULD. IEP goals are designed to answer a need, not raise questions.} *[end]*

The following letter was emailed to the Director of Pupil Personnel Services (Mrs. Lackey):

{On June 14th, I met with the CSE to address Blake's special education needs, most importantly his reading deficits. As he approaches tenth grade and is reading on a 4th grade level, I believe you will agree with me that this is an immediate priority. Identified as early as February 2000 by the district's own evaluators, Blake's reading impairment has never been appropriately addressed. Remedial reading programs, resource rooms, and a special education English class have failed to raise his reading proficiency to grade level or near grade level. His current IEP does not provide him with specific reading or written language remediation. Although it was not my responsibility to seek and pay for a comprehensive reading evaluation, I did so because it was clear that the IEP team needed a foundation upon which to build an appropriate IEP for my son.

The team agreed on June 14th that Dr. X's report was accurate and useful in planning for Blake's reading needs. As a result, the team offered to send Blake to a specialized school (Churchill, for example), stating they had your approval to do so. Moving Blake to such a restrictive environment would be at great cost to the district and to Blake. He is entitled to be in the least restrictive environment. Sending him away from his peers and denying him the opportunity to participate in a variety of school activities with his non-disabled peers would be a mistake. It is a moot point, however, because schools such as the one the team suggested have no openings at this late date.

The team then proposed a prescriptive English class which would include, by their own admission, students who are emotionally disturbed, failing all subjects, receiving counseling and strictly monitored for behavioral issues. As you are aware Blake's needs are not similar to these students' needs. In addition, this class was not designed to meet the intense reading instruction that Blake requires. A Wilson reading program was also offered by the IEP team three days a week in a group setting. Dr. X's evaluation expressly states that Blake requires intensive and individualized intervention which should begin immediately.

There has been a history of neglect on the district's part to Blake's reading impairment which I cannot allow to continue. I have paid for and scheduled the evaluation that was needed to help us plan to address his needs. I am requesting that the district work with me as we get the appropriate program in place for Blake. I am seeking your intervention in this matter because of the seriousness of it and the consequences for Blake. I have identified a Wilson trained tutor who will work with Blake over the summer with the plan, as Dr. X suggests, that this will move him along toward developing a new skill base upon which district staff could build in the fall. I view this as less costly for the district and for Blake. Thank you for your support of Blake.} *[end]*

Thank goodness Kay was at the meeting. Mr. Fuchs' main focus was the fact that I sent a lot of emails! When Mr. Fuchs came right out and said I was being abusive to the teachers, my frustration got the better of me. Unfortunately, this ended up being somewhat of a screaming match. I took great offense to being called abusive. (I will talk about this in a later chapter since the district made a major issue of my emails!) Kay put her hand on my knee to calm me down and she proceeded to get the meeting back on track. Though in reality, once again, not much was accomplished.

11

THE DECISION TO HIRE AN ATTORNEY

This was a decision I struggled with for months. It was one thing to have an advocate assist and support you at meetings, but I knew as soon as I hired an attorney, the atmosphere would become nasty.

The summer before Blake was to begin 10th grade, I found out the current Assistant Superintendent of Pupil Personnel Services (ASPPS) had just retired. It was also the reason why no one had responded to a letter I wrote asking for additional services. I immediately scheduled an appointment with the new Assistant Superintendent of Pupil Personnel Services.

We had that appointment in August. Mr. Jack (the AP who has been working with us also attended. Mrs. Lackey (the ASPPS) and I seemed to understand each other and promises were made to look into events, and make some changes, that would be in Blake's best interest. I was more hopeful after that meeting than ever before. This was also the first time Mr. Jack and Mrs. Lackey had met each other.

A CSE meeting was scheduled for September 27th. Though productive and long (I will address this issue at a later date), I felt a need for a follow up meeting because many of my concerns were still not addressed. I sent the following email to those that attended:

From: Elaine

Sent: Friday, September 28, 2007 11:03 AM

To: Mrs. Lackey, Mr. Jack, Mrs. Gilley, Ms. Abeles

Subject: meeting on 9/27/2007

Hi all! I want to thank you again for yesterday. It was one of the most positive meetings we have had ever! I know we need a follow up meeting because we did not get to finish going through everything, especially Blake's goals. I thought if I would put my thoughts on paper it might help to expedite the meeting.

The following may not be in any particular order. The IEP...

On pg. 1 -

1: The consultant teacher direct (which I believe would be Mrs. Gilley) needs to be changed to a frequency of 5.

2: I don't know what or who the CT Indirect is?

On pg. 2 -

3: Books on tape should be changed to books on CD/DVD as the tapes have been too difficult for Blake to utilize. On a side note, he has not been given these since 7th grade. For the summer reading this year he did use a CD that he was able to transfer on to his Ipod.

4: "Check for Understanding" needs to be asking Blake to explain back the directions. If you ask him if he understands he will usually tell you yes because he really does think he understands.

5: Assistive Tech Services - This area still concerns me, as I know there is technology that will help address his issue. Many were recently displayed at the NYC conference for the International Dyslexic Association. Kurzweil was one of them but there are now newer more efficient systems. At the meeting in June 2007, we all agreed that this should happen. Mr. Fuchs said that everyone was booked up and that it could not be done until 11/07. On page 15 of Dr. X's neoropsych report, she too recommends that Blake undergo an ATE. At this time, I would like to speak to whoever in the district administers the ATE so I can get additional information as to the process. I would like to do this asap.

6: Testing Accommodations - The following are items I would like to have added:

A - Spelling, Grammar, Punctuation waived. This item was on previous IEP's but was taken off this current one. The theory, as I was told, was that they don't really grade this way in the high school. I don't quite understand why that was said to me. Blake was definitely penalized on a variety of homework, tests and projects in 9th grade.

B: Possible use of a word bank when appropriate. Due to Blake's major spelling issues, sometimes what he writes is not what he means.

<u>On pg. 3 -</u>

7: Developing reading skills - This is the absolute root of Blake's problems. We still have not come up with plan that fits into Blake's schedule. Unfortunately, what was graciously offered (2-3 X week, 1:1, 8th period) will take away from his resource time, which I feel, and I believe everyone agrees, he will need in order to keep up with the current workload. At this time, I would again like to make a formal request for the district to pay for a private Wilson tutor outside of the regular school day.

8: Shouldn't it be noted anywhere, that the test results dated 1/19/2007 were from testing done privately? On a side note, I do want to reiterate that it was confirmed by Mrs. Rice and Mr. Fuchs in our June 2007 meeting and then again by Mrs. Rice at yesterday's meeting, that Blake's 8th grade testing was flawed and that the decoding piece was not done. I had been bringing up this issue since December 2005 and it was pretty much ignored.

9: Social Development - I don't understand why the comments listed under this category are listed under this category. Blake's "degree and quality of his relationships with peers adults, feelings about self and social adjustment to school and community environments" is extremely high. I see no problem with this at all. Blake's "ability to problem solve, work independently, develop coping skills" are all extremely high functioning except as it relates to academics, not social situations.

"The student needs to advocate for needs and be encouraged to make use of compensatory strategies." There are several problems with this statement:

A - Often times he does not think he needs help because he thinks, and is quite confident, that he is doing the task correctly.

B - Blake has been told so many things over the past 8 years that there is a high level of confusion as to what he has a right to expect. That confusion is not only from him but us as well. It also showed in yesterday's meeting when we had the discussion of what certain things meant, and there were a variety of opinions.

C - Blake has never been taught on a consistent basis these "compensatory" strategies. The main reason for this is that he has been told that he was not paying attention, he wasn't focusing, he was lazy, maybe he is ADD?, the list goes on. The owness was totally put on him, that all of this was his doing. As you well know, the issue of his Dyslexia has only begun being recently addressed. Blake needs to relearn all over again and this will take time. We also need to remember that Blake is consistently and competently reading on about a 5th grade level according to the Dr's report.

On pg. 4 -

10: 10: Transition Activities - Supposedly a level 1 vocational assessment was done. I was not aware of this and at the June 2007 meeting, Mr. Fuchs was suppose to send me a copy which I never received. I would like to know who did this assessment, what it involved and what the follow up would be. If in fact it was not done or not thorough, I would like to request an independent evaluation at the district's expense.

On pg. 6 -

11: Measurable goals - I specifically requested at the June 2007 meeting that Blake's goals not be written in percentages. None of the goals listed are measurable in this way. I would also like if we can evaluate more than just on a quarterly basis.

12: Study Skills: These seem to focus more on day to day homework which I see as quite different that study skills.

On pg. 7 -

13: Blake's computer use, I feel, should be under AT. It is not a goal, it is a necessity.

14: How does one measure "refocus when prompted"?

15: Reading: None of the goals listed are viable since there is no current reading program in place. They also seem arbitrary only working on 3 sounds.

16: Who would be working with him on the independent reading with questions and answers?

17: Career/Vocation/ Transition: Supposedly the Level 1 plan was already done so this seems to be a conflict.

On pg. 8 -

18: Blake can, now, indicate 2 areas of interests, strengths, and weaknesses. He will also tell you that whatever he does as a career will revolve around sports.

I hope you all find this helpful and I look forward to our next meeting. Thanks again for all your concern and cooperation.

Sincerely,

Elaine *[end of email]*

The following is Mrs. Lackey's response (or her lack of response to my very detailed email!)

RE: meeting on 9/27/2007

Monday, October 1, 2007 5:11 PM

From: "Mrs. Lackey"

To: Elaine, Mr. Jack, Mrs. Gilley, Mrs. Rice, Ms. Abeles

Hi, Elaine,

I'm glad you found the meeting to be positive. I appreciate your efforts along with the outstanding collaboration of Mr. Jack, Mrs. Gilley, Mrs. Rice and Blake's general education teachers.

I'll respond to the part below that pertains specifically to me. As I said in our meeting at the HS last week, the district has offered reading instruction that you did not use. Also to reiterate, the district will not pay for private or after-school tutoring.

Thank you, Mrs. Lackey *[end]*

It was Mrs. Lackey's response that started to put things into motion:

- Just to recap, did the district offer Blake a reading program? In theory, yes they did. Was it well thought out? No, it was not.

- Did Blake have room in his schedule for such a reading program? No, he did not.

- Did they give me last minute notice about a summer program (Thursday to start on Monday)? Yes, they did.

- Was it at a "special" school in the district where many of the students have social and behavioral issues? Yes, it was.

- Was it for an appropriate length of time? No, it was not.

- Did Blake already have a commitment for the summer? Yes he did.

- Did they tell me Blake should maybe drop ASL (a subject in which he was doing well) in order to take this reading program? Yes, they most certainly did.

It was my understanding, if a student needs services, he can't be denied based on whether or not he has room in his schedule.

At this point, the decision to hire an attorney was an easy one. I was tired of the long same old, same old meetings. On average, most of our meetings could last two to three hours! The topics and discussions were always the same. I had enough of them asking Blake (and I) to jump through hoops.

I read somewhere the definition of insanity was repeating the same actions over and over yet expecting different outcomes. It was time to change the game plan.

Through the help of my student advocate (Kay), I found our attorney, Andy Carter.

12

BLAKE'S SOPHOMORE YEAR

With the formal testing behind him and his issues now known and very specific, Blake's sophomore year should have been smooth sailing. There was no more guesswork. At this point, we all knew what needed to be done.

It did not take long before all that started to unravel.

ASL 3 – The teacher Blake was supposed to have was out on maternity leave (Mrs. Hirsch). The problem was this class had the same teacher for ASL in 8th grade. She was nice, but even back then; she could not control the class. Also, in 8th grade, she had gone out on maternity leave the second half of the year and only came back for the last few weeks. Mrs. Hirsch was expected to return in the 3Q. **This class, by the end of 10th grade would have had 6 ASL teachers, over a 4-year period**.

Mrs. Gallo was the sub. She did have a tough time in the beginning though, some of it, was not her fault. It was someone's brilliant idea to put both the level 3 and the level 4Honors in the same classroom, with the same teacher, learning at the same time. Initially, this was a disaster. However, Mrs. Gallo quickly took command of the class and the kids actually learned and liked what they were doing.

The first half of the year went well. Then Mrs. Hirsch came back. Many of us tried to get the administration to split the class since they now had two teachers. The students in level 3 that previously had Mrs. Hirsch would stay with Mrs. Gallo. It seemed like a perfect plan. We never even got an answer as to why this could not be done. We were ignored. Again, the district did not do what was in the best interest of the students.

Blake had an A- in 2nd Q with Mrs. Gallo and dropped to a C+ in 3Q with Mrs. Hirsch. This was typical of most of the level 3 students.

I was concerned with the drastic drop in grades. Based on some previous issues, I did email Mrs. Hirsch for a copy of Blake's grades. I also asked for an explanation of how she, in fact, graded. She did this. She also gave the class a chance to re-take some quizzes where the majority of the class did not do well. I became one of her major supporters. I believed she was trying.

Then, we got Blake's final grade and something just did not make sense. I pulled out all the paperwork and started to figure out his numbers, as per her instructions.

HER MATH WAS WRONG!! It took the next <u>10 months</u> and many meetings, just to have someone sit down with a calculator and a pencil, and spend 5 minutes to re-do the math. Blake's grade was eventually changed from a C+ to a B+!

There was never an apology (except from Mr. Jack - Assistant Principal) from the teacher or the head of the department. The Principal (Mr. Vick) made the grade change, but never acknowledged this was a huge problem.

TV Studio Production – One of the highlights of Blake's day.

Earth Science – Mr. Peter taught this class. He was a perfect match for Blake. He was the "cool" teacher with the tattoos, the band, and more importantly, the enthusiasm. Blake did not even mind going to his extra help because it was "not boring". Mr. Peter really wanted his students to learn and tried a variety of ways to keep them involved. One way was their edible projects, which they all got to share.

<u>*Mr. Peter was not hired back*</u>. He was just the latest in a series of teachers that were not re-hired the year after Blake had them. Again no one seemed to think this was a problem. Blake was really hoping to have Mr. Peter for Chemistry.

There was, however, a problem with the communication from the department. In May, I sent an email to find out the review schedule for the Regents Final Exam. I was told to go to the website. There in bold letters was a regents review schedule titled "**Midterm Review**" with **May** dates!

English 10 – This was what the district called a Co-Teach class. Basically Blake had one teacher he really liked and one that he didn't. The one teacher, Ms. Abeles, was great with Blake and really encouraged him. It also helped that she was not only smart but really nice too. Blake worked hard to please her. He would go to her room just to hang out and she would give him work to do. Her expectations for Blake were high and he would rise to the challenge.

Blake was still struggling with vocabulary. This was a never-ending battle. When I was helping him study for midterms, a friend's mom, whose son was in the self-contained class, told me his class was given a specific list of words. Some of them would be on the test. The difference was the amount of words they had to study.

After the midterms, I found out the self-contained students were also tested by given their vocabulary words in context. This seemed to make more sense to test Blake in this manner since he struggled so much with vocabulary. Originally, they told me they could not do that because Blake was not in self-contained. I asked if the point of the exam was to see if the students knew the words or to see if they can take a test. This argument went back and forth for weeks.

I also found out one of the modifications I could ask for was to have Blake tested one on one. This was a modification they did not want to give me. When Blake had a reader, they were in a group setting, which meant they basically read to the slowest person in the group. That was one of the reasons Blake needed extra time. What ended up happening was Blake would become frustrated and bored. They finally compromised and said the modification would only be used for exams over 45 minutes, as in midterms and finals. A small battle was won.

Below is an actual copy of an assignment that was given about Julius

Caesar. There are a few items circled. The quality of the scan is not great and I only included the items in question, but you will clearly get an idea of why I was so upset. And this was from the English Dept...

ﬆus Caesar Review Worksheet ACT II

ETTING ACQUAINTED WITH THE CHARACTERS IN *JULIUS CAESAR*

In your first lesson dealing with *Julius Caesar*, the questions were designed to help you understand the plot and ﬆing of the play. The second lesson emphasized certain qualities of three important characters: Caesar, Cassius, and ﬆrk Antony. Act II focuses on the fourth major character, Brutus, but it also acquaints you with the two wives, ﬅpurnia and Portia, and reveals new facets of Caesar's makeup.

ﬆer reading the summary of Act II and Act II itself, you should be able to answer the following questions:

1. In Act II, Scene I, Brutus envies his young servant who is sleeping so soundly. Portia, Brutus's wife, comments later in this scene that Brutus got up in the night, left the bedroom, and did not return. What is the apparent cause of Brutus's restlessness and inability to sleep?

   That he is nervous + that he is hiding something.

2. Since Brutus has not personal grudge against Caesar, what must he convince himself before he can take a part in Caesar's assassination? What is Brutus' tragic flaw as illustrated in this soliloquy?

   is that he is weak + not fit to be king.

3. At this point, what adjectives would you use to describe Brutus's character?

   Persuasive, arrogant.

4. Cassius, unlike Brutus, is partly motivated by personal dislike of Caesar. What do you think in the underlying cause of this dislike?

   is that he has more power.

   1. The contrast between Brutus and Antony's speech to the people in regards to Caesar's death is _____ *Brutus has no evidence* _____. Antony's method for swaying the people is using the repetition of Brutus being _____ *honorable* _____ and Caesar being _*Ambitous*_____. In addition, his speech is an example of *verbal* _____ and _*dramatic*_ irony because _we know his anger_____.

   10. _*Octavius*_ is coming to Rome because *Ceasar wrote him a letter* He will join forces with Antony to seek revenge for Caesar's death. Caesar's spirit cannot be _*put to rest*_ until _*revenge*_____.

   11. Antony proves to be _____ when he convinces the conspirators he is on their side. He gives them his word when he _*shakes his bloody hand*_. His only request to Brutus is to _*Cassius*_ and despite _*Cassius*_ warning, Brutus grants him permission under certain conditions. These are _*An tisaoes is ___ in this talk*_, and _*stand to say sects*_. Brutus's biggest mistake of all was _____. He did this because he _*left*_.

   12. _____ reveals his internal conflict in his *honorable* . He claims he has no _____ cause to turn against Caesar except for _____. He thinks it is possible Caesar will _____; however, the problem with this rationalization is _____. The determining factor that finalizes his decision is _____.

For those that may be wondering...I did, indeed, return it to the teacher, the head of the department and the Assistant Principal, with all the mistakes circled in **RED**! I was adamant, about the fact, if Blake would have turned in something with this many errors, he would have been told to re-check his work and re-write it.

I also included a copy of The Columbia Guide to Standard American English 1993 referencing the use of *"in regards to"*: *"... In regards to*, however, is both Substandard and Vulgar, although it appears unfortunately often in the spoken language of some people who otherwise use Standard. It never appears in Edited English."

No one seemed to think this was a problem either.

Math Sequential 2 – Let me explain what this is. I don't know how it is in other states but in New York, they keep changing the curriculum and coming up with non-descriptive names. Blake took the first 2/3 of Math A in 9th grade. He took the last 3rd of Math A during the first half of 10th grade and then took the NYS Math A Regents Exam. The 2nd half of 10th grade was the first 3rd of Math B. If it is confusing for you, you can imagine how the students and parents felt.

My oldest daughter had the same teacher. He was wonderful for her but not for Blake. Blake had a very difficult time with his Asian accent and also with his handwriting. Though Mr. Louie was more than willing to try and help, it was problematic to overcome these obstacles.

Below is a copy of an actual worksheet that was given to the entire class. It was also indicative of many of the worksheets during year.

Elaine Mellon

/ Course 2 Key   hwk #5   Due 2/4/08 m

name: ①

   For each of the following do   a) find discriminant
                                  b) nature of roots
                                  c) roots using Quadratic formula

1) $4x^2 - x - 3 = 0$ a) $1 + 48 = 49$

                        b) real, rational, + unequal

                        c) $\dfrac{1 \pm \sqrt{49}}{8} = \dfrac{1 \pm 7}{8} = \left(1, \dfrac{-3}{4} \right)$

2) $x^2 + 4x - 1 = 0$ a) $16 + 4 = 20$

                        b) real, irrational, + unequal

                        c) $\dfrac{-4 \pm \sqrt{20}}{2} = \dfrac{-4 \pm 2\sqrt{5}}{2} = \boxed{-2 \pm \sqrt{5}}$

3) $x^2 + 3x + 9 = 0$ a) $9 - 36 = -27$

                        b) imaginary

                        c) $\dfrac{-3 \pm \sqrt{-27}}{2} = $ no Real Roots

4) $4x^2 + 4x + 1 = 0$ a) $16 - 16 = 0$ ②
   b) real, rational, + equal
   c) $\dfrac{-4 \pm \sqrt{0}}{8} = \left(-\dfrac{1}{2}, -\dfrac{1}{2} \right)$

5) $5x^2 + 4x - 13 = 0$ (Round ans to nearest tenth)
   a) $16 + 260 = 276$
   b) real, irrational, + unequal
   c) $\dfrac{-4 \pm \sqrt{276}}{10} = \left(1.3, -2.1 \right)$

6) if the roots are imaginary, give 2 examples of what the discriminant might be   Ex. -27, -3

7) if the roots are real, rational, unequal, give 2 examples of what the discriminant might be   Ex. 25, 16

8) Write the equation if you're given these roots
   a) $\{3, -1\}$
   $x - 3 = 0$ $x + 1 = 0$
   $(x - 3)(x + 1) = 0$
   ~~$x^2 + x = 0$~~
   $x^2 - 2x - 3 = 0$

   b) $\{4, -2\}$
   $x - 4 = 0$ $x + 2 = 0$
   $(x - 4)(x + 2) = 0$
   $x^2 - 2x - 8 = 0$

   c) $\{\frac{3}{4}, 2\}$
   $x - \frac{3}{4} = 0$ $x - 2 = 0$
   $(4x - 3) = 0$ $(x - 2) = 0$
   $4x^2 - 8x - 3x + 6 = 0$
   $4x^2 - 11x + 6 = 0$

9) Simplify: $\dfrac{18 \pm 9\sqrt{3}}{6} = \dfrac{6 \pm 3\sqrt{3}}{2}$

10) Simplify: $\dfrac{4 \pm 12\sqrt{2}}{4} = 1 \pm 3\sqrt{2}$

Blake's final grade for math was a D+.

Resource Room – This is another program that needs explanation. Officially, it is a class where the students are supposed to be working on their IEP goals and objectives. Unofficially, it is a study hall. The Resource Room teacher is "supposed" to be keeping track of progress made. They are also to keep in touch with the teachers and be a liaison between the parent and staff.

One of my consistent complaints was I often had to contact several teachers, repeating myself either through emails or phone calls. Email was the easier way to do this. What I preferred was, to have a contact person in the school that had easier access to the teachers. This should have been the Resource Room teacher, who for Blake was Mrs. Gilley. As much as she tried, she had too many students to look out for and not enough support.

My first contact with Mrs. Gilley was a form letter that she sent to all the parents in September. Instead of re-writing her letter she had obviously been using for years, Mrs. Gilley sent it unsigned, not dated and with several lines sloppily crossed out in pencil. This did not make a good first impression!

Fortunately, Mrs. Gilley was supportive of Blake. She was patient, which was a great help.

Blake made the JV Basketball team and had practice almost every day. He lived for basketball! In order for him to stay on the team and continue to play, he had to be in school every day, for at least five periods. This was a major motivating factor, but I was concerned about how he would handle his schoolwork and practice.

Mrs. Gilley quickly realized something I already knew, something that was mentioned on most of his IEPs (Individual Education Plan). Blake had no study skills to speak of. His time management was inconsistent at best. If he said a task was only going to take an hour or so, we knew it would take much longer. His organizational skills were non-existent. How could these still be issues year after year after year?

Global History – Mrs. Manna was a great teacher and loved the subject matter. She taught a Self-contained class. This class was supposed to be exactly the same as a regular class but with fewer students, more modifications and more support. Unfortunately, very often, this type of class has many issues, usually a slower level and behavior problems. Blake had none of these, but since he was having a hard time with the material, it was the only solution the district had. Basically Global History (as I said earlier), forgive the pun, but many of the names and places were foreign to him.

I asked Mrs. Manna if she could tutor Blake. After all, he would go to her anyway for extra help and also during Resource Room. In an email she responded, "I cannot tutor a student outside of school in a subject that I currently have that student in. In other words, I can't tutor [Blake] in global because he is in my class. It's a district policy, and they take it very seriously. I wish I could because it is my favorite subject to tutor." I get that she would be getting paid as a tutor but my taxes are paying her anyway as a teacher. So either way I am paying. I don't see it as a conflict. If she were the best at what she does then I would want to hire the best as a tutor. The only one who lost out was Blake.

Mrs. Manna and Mrs. Gilley worked very well together and Blake definitely benefitted from them.

13

PART 1:
WE NEED HELP. ENTER THE LAWYER.

The Student Advocate that had been helping us was extremely frustrated with how the district was treating, not only Blake, but me as well. She suggested it might be time to move on to the next step. Over the next few months, I researched various attorneys, their experience, their fees, and their references. I had consultations with several firms in person and by phone, sometimes both. It was going to cost us quite a bit of money and nothing is guaranteed. I was also worried about what the fallout could possibly be.

The fall semester of Blake's sophomore year, as shown in the previous chapter, was not very productive. Midterm week was worse! It was the last straw and I made a decision that would affect my family for the next twelve months.

Below is the actual email I sent to the attorney. As you read it, you will see what other nonsense Blake had to deal with (see "On Friday" paragraph!) and why it was completely clear something needed to be done.

Thursday, January 31, 2008 11:20 AM

Hi! Sorry it has taken a bit to get back to you. We wanted to get through midterm week (See below) and we also had Blake retested at a Sylvan Learning Center. My husband wanted him tested "cold" without the tester knowing anything about Blake's history and it confirmed what we already knew. We are considered enrolling him in their program to get him the reading help he needs.

Our plan is to send out a check and the contract to you on Saturday so we can get this ball rolling.

Some interesting events happened during midterm week:

Global 1Q	B-	2Q C	Semester C	midterm exam 58
English	B-	C	C	70
Science	A	B	B	74
Math	D+	C	C	84 Math A Regents!!!

How do you get a D+ and C's but pull an 84 on the regents?? A very good tutor!

On Monday when there was no school, a friend of mine who's son is in the intensive class for English told me they got a vocabulary list of 35 words, 25 of which were on the test and that the intensive test was going to be different than the regular. I went crazy because it has been shoved down our throats that the intensive is the same just a smaller class. Blake is in a co-teach class as one of the few special education students. I sent an email to the immediate world that I would be in the guidance office at 8am and someone needed to come find me and explain. The principal came in at 9:30 (the test was from 8-10) and explained the difference in the exams and I said it was not acceptable to change the rules midway through. He agreed and had them find Blake's English teacher so she can go up and work with him and go over the vocabulary the same as the intensive.

On Friday, Blake was supposed to take his Earth Science midterm. He went to the testing center (he was taking all his midterms 1:1) filled out the booklet and was leafing through the test and was starting to panic because nothing looked familiar. About 5 minutes or so into the testing when he couldn't answer any of the questions, he realized that **they had given him the Bio midterm instead of the Earth Science!!** No one seems to think that this was a big deal...

I met with the woman who was supposed to do the Assistive Technology evaluation for Blake because I wanted to see what they had. After meeting with her (she was very nice) we decided that she didn't even need to meet with Blake for now because there were a few things that I thought he should try. I didn't want to overwhelm him. These programs would be for him to use at home: Kurzweil Version 10, Lexia, Text Help Read and Write.

I put in a formal request to Mrs. Rice (HS Sp. Ed) for the district to provide Blake with a laptop with wireless capabilities. She forwarded the request to Mr. Fuchs and Mrs. Lackey.

Respectfully submitted,

Elaine *[end]*

13

PART 2:
THE HEARINGS

PRE HEARING - THE OVERVIEW

I need to start this section with just a brief (I use that term loosely) explanation because the details can get quite overwhelming. For those that want more information, I will try to provide them in as concise a way as possible. When you read this, it will make more sense. I will also provide some actual letters and responses where appropriate.

After my research, and on the suggestion of our Student Advocate, we hired Mr. Carter as our attorney of record. Mr. Carter is from Northwest, NY, a good 7+hours from us. He came highly recommended; his fees were less than those in NYC. His office was small so I knew I would be dealing with him rather than his interns. He was also willing to travel.

There was paperwork that needed to be filed with the district notifying them of the impending lawsuit. This was done in February. A Resolution Session was held on March 4th. We tried to waive our rights to this session because I felt we had said all we needed to say. The meeting was mostly unproductive. Mrs. Lackey, over and over, told us how much experience she had (30+ years) and that my requests were unreasonable. She said, "in all her years I have never seen anything like this." It was becoming increasingly obvious Mrs. Lackey was totally frustrated with me.

On April 17th, I received a letter from Mrs. Lackey. Highlights from the letter are below.

1-The Assistive Technology evaluation report was completed. Supposedly all recommended software had been ordered.

2- *"We [district] agreed that Blake needed to be assessed to determine at what level his Wilson reading instruction should begin. The results of the evaluation do not indicate Wilson reading instruction for Blake. Please see attached report. Nevertheless, I again offer to provide it to Blake as a courtesy because of your strong interest in it. [end]*

The report (signed by two of the Special Ed teachers, one being Mrs. Manna, Blake's Global teacher) attached to the above letter was dated April 16th and said the testing was done on April 2nd and 8th. In the letter, no specific scores were given to us. There were no details.

The letter stated: *The Results of the test indicate that he [Blake] would not be an appropriate candidate for the Wilson Reading Program. His scores were also compared with the WADE scores of the students currently enrolled in Wilson. Blake's were found to be much higher overall. This would indicate that the program would not significantly improve his skills.*

I proceeded to fire off several emails to Mrs. Lackey, the Principal, the AP, the special ed teachers, and the attorneys saying I wanted to see the specific results of the testing and even to see the testing itself. I was not about to take their word over the hospital's Head of the Neuropsych Dept. Several emails went back and forth. I am including the emails because they have to be read to be believed.

From: Elaine

Sent: Wed 4/30/2008 7:27 AM

To: teachers; Mr. Jack

Subject: Wilson

Good morning! The letter I received last week regarding Blake's Wilson Assessment was surprisingly very non-descript. Can you please let me know:

1 - exactly how he scored

2 - exactly how he compared to the others presently taking the class

3 - if he were to start Wilson , at what level/book would he start

Thanks

Elaine *[end]*

Mrs. Lackey wrote:

Hi, Mrs. Mellon, Discussion about Wilson assessment and instruction will likely take place during the impartial hearing process. Thank you, Mrs. Lackey *[end]*

From: Elaine

Sent: Wednesday, April 30, 2008 3:19 PM

To: Lackey

Cc: same as above

Subject: RE: Wilson

Is there a reason I can't know before? It is a simple answer to a simple question. I don't understand the secrecy. Please explain. Thanks, Elaine *[end]*

Mrs. Lackey wrote:

Hi, Mrs. Mellon,

We are in litigation in the form of an impartial hearing. You might want to bring it up during the hearing. Thank you, Mrs. Lackey *[end]*

Date: Wed, 30 Apr 2008 13:23:19 -0700 (PDT)

From: Elaine

Subject: RE: Wilson

To: Mrs. Lackey

CC: Principal, Mrs. House, Mrs. Manna, Mrs. Rice, Mr. Jack, Mrs. Rock (School's attorney 1 of 2), School's Hired Law Firm

First, the hearings haven't begun and Second, even if they did, Blake's scores themselves have nothing to do with the hearing. He was tested and I want the scores. The letter sent to me was unacceptable without numbers. Your not giving me the scores is totally unethical and I should have had them immediately after the testing was completed on the April 9th. I should not have had to ask for them.

You were the one that said you did not want this to become adversarial yet you are causing the adversity.

I would appreciate an explanation other that we are in litigation. I have been nothing except open and honest with you and I expect the same.

Elaine *[end]*

I did not receive any paperwork until the first hearing, after we had to ask for it, again.

A Consent Decree was sent in April stating if the district did not agree with our requests, we would go directly to the hearings. I had all the proof we would need. They did not agree to most of our requests, which is what we expected. The first hearing was scheduled. Finally someone impartial was going to hear what we had to say, hear what we have been through, and hold the district accountable. Or so I thought…

We wanted the following (again this is the uncomplicated, informal version):

1 - To be reimbursed for Blake's Neuropsychological testing that was done outside the school district, which you should know cost me $4000 and was not covered by insurance. *(The district will claim at a later date, that I should not be reimbursed for these expenses because*

*I did not specifically tell them, **in writing**, that I wanted to have him tested outside the district. Even though there were numerous emails, phone calls and meetings regarding the botched 8th grade assessment!)*

2 - Blake needed to be in the Wilson Reading Program and I wanted them to provide this either after school or in the evening and pay for the tutor. He did not have, presently or in the past, room in his schedule.

3 - I wanted accountability on the part of the district for their egregious mistakes and oversights. Two of the major issues were:

> A - Omitting the decoding piece on his 8th grade testing and then sending me an incorrect report with major mistakes.

> B - Failure to implement meaningful and measurable goals and objectives. Blake's IEP was not an "**individual** educational plan".

4 - To be reimbursed for a good part of Blake's tutoring expenses, including, but not limited to, his tuition for Huntington Learning Center. I was told during the hearing "It is not uncommon for parent's in this district to hire tutors for their children."

Important Note: The statute of limitations in a lawsuit such as this is only two years. I was not permitted to address any issues for the years K - 7.

To put this into perspective, this is now taking place toward the end of Blake's sophomore year. It was now fifteen months since he was diagnosed with Developmental Dyslexia!

Outside of academics, Blake was now involved with the track team and was gearing up for a summer sports trip to Europe. Blake was one of several students selected to play basketball and represent the United States, as a People to People Sports Ambassador, at the International Youth Festival in Vienna, Austria.

I have a 4-inch binder filled with Blake's life since before kindergarten. Fortunately, I am a pack rat, and in the beginning, I saved most everything he drew, wrote, and painted. I did the same for my girls. As the years went by, my girls had issues with some of their paperwork. When something seemed "off" with Blake, I began to not only collect, but also arrange the paperwork in some semblance of order. It was what I would call an organized mess.

The first hearing was scheduled for April 28th. We were well prepared. My husband and I took off from work. Mr. Carter drove more than seven hours to meet us. **When we arrived at the district offices, we are told the hearing had been postponed!** They said they informed Mr. Carter, but were unclear as to how they tried to contact him. They never contacted us.

Over the next five months, we were subjected to **nine** days of hearings. (Two of which we needed to reschedule in order to deal with a family emergency. We notified them in more than enough time.) This alone was abusive and took its toll financially. After all, I had to take time off from work. I also felt like I was paying double because the school attorneys (there were two representing the district) were being paid with our very high, school taxes. So here I was paying the people we were suing. How messed up is that?

We did not have a single hearing that started on time. Most days the scheduled start time was not until 9:30 or 10am and often, started 10-20 minutes late. Once it even started 30 minutes late! There was an hour for lunch and usually by 3:30 or 4, it was over. For most people, that is not a full workday. For my husband, it is more like a half-day.

On May 28th, during the course of the hearings, I received the following letter from Mrs. Lackey (Assistant Superintendent for Pupil Services):

"It has become evident that your incessant communications are negatively impacting certain District employees in their ability to meet all of their obligations.

While it is clear that School District personnel have an obligation to answer reasonable requests for information about a child's progress, it is not required by any law, rule, or regulation of which I am aware that they must respond to incessant inquiries to the extent that their professional duties are neglected.

Therefore, please be advised that, effectively immediately, you will continue to be regularly informed as to your child's progress by his teachers. Any requests for information beyond that should be communicated by letter to me, not to Mr. Jack [Asst Principal] or to Blake's teachers." [end]

On June 2nd, Mr. Carter (our attorney) sent the following email to the district's attorney:

"My client received a letter today from [Mrs. Lackey]. It appears as if your client is retaliating against the parent due to her advocacy efforts on behalf of her child with a disability. As you likely are aware, this is a violation of both Section 504 and the ADA. It also seems as if your client is opening itself up to liability under Section 1983. We are putting you on notice, through this email.

Thank you for your attention to this matter.

Very truly yours," [end]

Mrs. Lackey's letter was in response to the ASL matter mentioned earlier. I paid no attention to her and carried on my business as usual. I was not going to be strong-armed or intimidated by anyone. To give you a better image of Mrs. Lackey, she stands over 6 feet tall with salt and pepper hair. She would have this way of standing and looking down over you when speaking to her. I actually found it quite amusing, but could easily see how she would try using her size to her advantage.

LET THE HEARINGS BEGIN – DAY 1 (MAY 1ST)

With over 1000 pages of testimony, you can imagine most of it was extremely boring, cumbersome, and redundant. What I want to try and do is bring out some of the highlights, in the order of their occurrence. I will also quote specific testimony when possible.

The hearings were to take place in the district offices, in one of their conference rooms. Let me introduce you to the players that were to be in attendance on most days: Me (Elaine - Mom), Charles - Dad, Mr. Carter - our attorney, Mrs. Rock & Mr. Waters - School's attorneys, Mrs. Orange - the "impartial" Hearing Officer, the transcriber, and Mrs. Lackey - Assistant Superintendent of Pupil Services.

I will be adding my side bar explanations to refute their comments or give further explanation. These will be in *italics*. The transcripts have not been altered or edited for spelling, grammar or punctuation mistakes. I have only included transcripts that were relevant, but have not distorted the content. Some of my reactions will appear toward the end of the hearings, since I had to "wait my turn" to comment. For the purpose of Blake's story, I felt this was a better use of the reader's time.

For those that want to skim through the transcripts, if you read the *italics*, it will give you a good sense of what is happening. Some of what will be said has been mentioned in previous chapters. I wanted to show how it came out during the testimony. It makes the case of how meaningless the process was.

Day 1 (May 1st):

Waters: As far as I have been able to determine, and I have verified this as recently as yesterday, he has never failed a course either in elementary school or in high school. The special education services that the child receives under his current IEP are significant and they are meeting with success.

Blake had failed classes in the past, but if he was not passing, the district's answer was to enter him into a lower level class. When this is done, the original failing grade is wiped off the transcript. Though it was not done for Blake in 9th grade, it was in 10th and 11th.

Waters: While it is not my intention to criticize any parent's desire to obtain the best services they can for their child I believe that when you have reviewed the testimony and the records in this case you will conclude that the parents incessant demands for changes in the child's services were well beyond the role of a parent and working with the school district cooperatively to craft an appropriate education.

There were hundreds of emails sent by me and to me over the two to three year periods. Often, it was just to say thanks for responding. However, if a teacher did not respond, another was sent.

<u>Waters</u>: **I truly believe as my mother instructed me when I was a very young child that there are some people that wouldn't be happy in heaven.**

Yes, you did read that right! This was the attitude of their attorneys. It was obvious their first order of business was to try and discredit me. They were not there to do what was in Blake's best interest. Their primary mission was to make me go away.

<u>Waters</u>: In this case the child's parents have functioned and participated as equal members of the school's IEP team. The proof will somehow show that they have apparently believed they were more than members of that team when they sought to unilaterally control all aspects of the child's education. They apparently believe that every decision taken by the school district's educators were and are subject to their demand for instant change if they disagreed with those decisions. They sought to control incomplete detail not only what was sought but when and by whom. They likewise sought veto power over methodology employed in every aspect of this child's education, and they demanded the absolute right to require that the school district stop providing services that the parents themselves had originally demanded.

I didn't seek "Unilateral control" but I did seek to have discussions on whether or not certain aspects were appropriate. I didn't seek "veto power over methodology employed in EVERY aspect". I did seek to have discussions on whether those "methodologies" were in Blake's best interest. We stopped services that were not working.

<u>Mrs. Rice</u>: Head of Special Ed in the high school is now testifying:

Rice: The student's mother requested an increase in special education services (for bio) as she believed he required a more restrictive and supportive program and to meet his academic potential.

I never "requested an increase in Spec Ed services", I asked for help because his bio teacher was ineffective.

Waters to Rice:

Q: The child's mother attended and if I read this correctly requested that her son be placed in a self-contained special English class, is that accurate?"

A: And social studies class at that time.

Q: Was that done?

A: It was done.

*Again, I never requested this. **They** suggested I change Blake's placement. This is the first time I found out there even was an Intensive Global but Blake had lost so much time, it was recommended he go into the self-contained. They all raved about the teacher and said he would be good for Blake. No other suggestions were made. The only option I was given was to put him in that class.*

Waters to Rice:

Q: If I read this IEP correctly it was you who recommended that the student might benefit from Wilson reading, is that correct?

A: Well, I think very highly of the program and I did, I did feel that at the time that I recommended it I think that, I just need to mention this, we did not have any data, any documentation that indicated that there was a decoding problem. But mom reported it. And mom reported it that it had been a concern in previous years. We offered it at that time without the documentation at the end of an IST meeting.

They didn't have any data??? What about the 2nd, 5th, and 8th grade testing they did? They did not do the decoding in 8th grade! I definitely was not "offered" Wilson at the IST meeting. Actually, Mrs. Rice specifically told me the program had already started and it was too late for him to go into it. She also stated, it is primarily juniors and seniors that take the program.

Rice: So we felt that we, at that time, at that meeting, we did offer to provide more testing because we didn't, we didn't have the documentation. And we also offered the Wilson program.

They did not offer more testing. In fact, Mrs. Rice told me "there was nothing else to test for!"

Rice: Well, I would have to double check, but at that time the documentation that we were using was not indicative of someone who was in need of Wilson reading program.

Their documentation was flawed. Remember the 8ᵗʰ grade School Psychologist? The contents below are taken exactly from a note and a letter, she sent to me: Hand written note - " Sorry about the miss type of his observation." Typed letter - " I am sending you a new copy of Blake's report because I finally realized what happened and made the proper corrections...I accidently copied and pasted my observation write-up for last year into this year's report.... To be honest, I still did not feel that the report was right. It was haunting me."

As Day 1 was ending, we once again asked for the results of Blake's Wilson testing. I was handed a piece of paper. There was no name on it. The top 2/3 was blank and there were some scores on the bottom. Mrs. Lackey chuckled as she gave it to me and said we have to trust her that, it was indeed, Blake's test results. We never did see the originals and NO I did not trust her.

HEARINGS - DAY 2 (MAY 5TH)

Today, the District brought in Mrs. Manna. She was Blake's 9th grade self-contained English teacher for the second half of the year and his Intensive Global teacher for 10th grade.

WATERS TO MANNA:

Q: The student was offered a Wilson Reading program. Was the Wilson Reading program offered again at this meeting?

A: It was discussed.

Q: I would ask you to look at the latter part of the third paragraph?

A: Okay.

Q: Does that comport with your recollection?

A: Yes.

Q: Who was it that offered the Wilson Reading program, if you remember?

A: recall Mr. Fuchs offering the Wilson Reading program.

Q: Do you remember what the response to that offer was?

A: I remember there was discussion because there was some concern about whether or not it would fit in his schedule with his ASL class and also I believe the television production class, is my recollection.

The Wilson program was never offered; it was only discussed.

WATERS TO MANNA AND CARTER:

Q: Does Blake get books on tape?

A: Blake does get books on tape as part of this IEP, yes.

Q: How about in your class?

A: We only have one major textbook and we don't actually use it all that much.

Q: Now, is it part --

Carter: May we have an answer to the last question?

Waters: She got an answer.

Hearing Officer: No, the question was on tape and she just said we have one that's not used very much, but she didn't say whether or not he has it on tape.

Waters: All right.

Q: Does he have it on tape?

A: No, Blake does not have the book on tape. Sorry.

Q: Why is that?

A: I don't know.

This does not even need an explanation! A good part of today's hearing was again the amount of emails I had sent. Mrs. Manna noted that several of the emails were to thank her for her help and also to keep her in the loop of how Blake was doing. Waters kept asking about Blake's willingness to go to extra help. Sometimes he went. Maybe he could have gone more often but his frustration was getting the best of him.

WATERS TO MANNA:

Q: Please look at 45? What is 45?

A: It's an e-mail from Blake. He wanted to know how he did on his previous exam. And he had a basketball game; so he was asking if he could come to my eighth period study hall and put his notebook together there, help him organize it.

Q: Do you remember whether he did?

A: Yes, he did.

I had often heard that Blake needed to "advocate for himself". This was a perfect example, how in certain circumstances, he was able to accomplish this. When he was with a teacher that was positive and encouraging, it brought out the best in him. Mrs. Manna was one of those teachers that really cared for her students.

CARTER TO MANNA:

Q: You're not aware of him getting any Wilson instruction this school year?

A: No, I am not.

Q: Are you aware of him attending the Huntington Learning Center?

A: No, I was not, am not.

Q: Now, in regard to District Exhibit 16, these myriad e-mails, many of those were initiated by you, right?

A: Yes.

Q: And did you believe it inappropriate if Miss Mellon responded back to e-mails --

A: No, I do not.

Q: -- that you send? And do you know how many e-mails, individual e-mails Miss Mellon sent you?

A: I did not.

Q: Do you think it was too many?

A: I think it was excessive, yes, in some cases, yes.

Q: I'd ask you to turn to District Exhibit 16?

A: Okay.

Q: Which is the batch of e-mails?

A: Okay.

Q: And if you would take some time and point out to us those which you think were sent and addressed in an unreasonable topic for a parent to be communicating with a special education teacher of their child?

Waters: Objection, that's not her testimony, that a topic was inappropriate. She testified that the number of e-mails was excessive, not the topics.

Carter: I'll rephrase the question.

Q: Can you point to any e-mail that you think is an indication that the e-mail itself was not warranted to be communicated between you and the parent?

A: Could I ask you to rephrase that? I'm sorry, I'm not sure exactly what type of answer you're looking for. I'm sorry.

Q: Okay. I suppose we can go through them one by one. Let's start in the back with --

HO: I'm going to object to taking the time to go through 102. So can we try and rephrase the question one more time?

Q: Is there any e-mail in there that you think was inappropriate for Mrs. Mellon to communicate with you about Blake?

A: No.

Again, Waters is continuing to attack about emails and not really focusing on Blake. I felt terrible for Manna because she is a great teacher and they were trying to twist her words. It was obvious someone had "unofficially coached" the teachers because several of them used the same exact phrases during their testimony.

The following excerpt deals with one of Blake's IEP goals I thought was ridiculous. It states, "Blake will bring his homework home 75% of the time." I argued that this was not measurable. It did not matter how often he brought home his homework but rather how often he turned in the homework.

CARTER TO MANNA:

Q: Did you respond to Mrs. Mellon's query about the goal on the IEP?

A: I did not respond to that, no.

Q: Is Blake only required to turn in his homework 75 percent of the time?

A: No, he's not, not in my class.

Q: How was this goal developed?

A: I was not part of the development of this goal.

Q: How often does Blake turn in his homework?

A: About 90 to 95 percent of the time, I would say, in my class.

Q: And has that been relatively consistent all year, 90, 95 percent of the time?

A: It has improved greatly since January. So it's closer to 100 percent in the second half of the year.

A: Blake seems to struggle with some of the reading of the more higher level documents that are a part of global history assessment. Primary documents like old journals from the French revolution or sometimes with maps. And he often will ask me to reiterate what is stated on those types of things, so I see where he struggles.

CARTER TO MANNA:

Q: And correct me if I'm wrong but you previously testified that the Committee on Special Education had determined that the Wilson was an appropriate program for Blake?

A: I did.

All of the above happened before lunch. After lunch, Mrs. Gilley was called in. She was Blake's Resource Room teacher and also his IEP teacher.

Gilley: I have a teaching assistant for the most part who is a certified -- actually he's not certified, he is a college graduate.

WATERS TO GILLEY:

Q: Now, I've copied 191 e-mails that have come from your file. **Is that an usual number of e-mails that you have with a parent?**

A: No.

Even after getting this answer from Gilley, Waters still needs to go on and on trying to back her into a corner: trying to get the answer he was hoping for.

<u>Gilley:</u> "I've witnessed Blake using his agenda book occasionally."

This is May. Blake has not used an agenda book since October!

<u>Gilley:</u> I don't have a checklist. Right, I don't do percentages per se."

The following is the list given to Blake to read so he could "master" one of his IEP goals. Remember Blake is in 10th grade!

<u>Gilley:</u> There were two lists. Given a list of ten words Blake will orally identify the rules for word attack skills regarding R control vowel sounds and read the words. The words, the ten words were rat, park, Lord, rib, rash, run, rot, rush, rag, rod. And that was taken from the Wilson Reading system. And then the other ten words, given a list of ten words that contain soft and hard C or soft and hard G, B. will decode the words. Ice, local, clothes, coma, adverse, illustrate, giraffe, gate, gave, genius, great. These were taken also from the Wilson Reading.

Q: He's mastered the two reading goals that the district has devised for him?

A: Correct.

Q: When did he master those 20 words?

A: On February 13th, '08."

The Neuropsychologist will testify, at a later date, as to how absurd it was to give this list to a 10th grader. The words are really for grades 1-3!

HEARINGS - DAY 3 (MAY 14TH)

Today's hearing featured Mr. Jack, the Assistant Principal. He was the one that had been extremely helpful. He often felt frustrated because his hands were tied. Mr. Jack was visibly pained during the day's proceeding and I felt for him because he was clearly between a rock and a hard place.

At the beginning, the School's attorney was trying to make it sound like I was badgering Mr. Jack. His testimony eventually stated this was not the case.

The District was claiming there were a total of approximately 333 pages of emails, over approximately a two-year period, involving Mr. Jack. Again, they were trying to insinuate I was abusing the system. They refused to acknowledge that some emails were CCs, some were just FYIs and some were just to say thanks. There were even a few that had nothing to do with Blake.

Q: Did you ever mention to Mrs. Mellon that the quantity of her e-mails is becoming or had become burdensome or excessive?

A: No.

Q: And if you can tell us why did you not mention this to Mrs. Mellon?

A: I absolutely know from my own experience as an assistant principal previous to [*this district*], so I've been doing this type of work for over, about 13 years now I would say, that a lack of communication makes things a lot worse than communication. So I really, really, really wanted constant communication to make sure that everything was understood in this situation. Plus I had many, many teachers who were very worried since they were non-tenured that they were going to be in trouble because of a lot of things that Mrs. Mellon was saying about grades and other things that were going on in those classes. So I absolutely needed to know everything she was saying so that I could make sure I was communicating to them effectively also. I also really believe that the door has to be open in communication. So if you have to have excessive communication for an assistant principal then you need to do that.

Also at this hearing, the attorneys tried to make it sound like I argued each grade Blake ever received. I did, in fact, question several grades and several tests as well, for good reason. In an earlier chapter, I noted how there were a number of times report card grades were wrong. There were tests and papers where the numbers did not add up. There were comments that did not make any sense. There were directions that were not clear. According to Blake's IEP "Directions are to be SPECFIC." This not only happened to Blake, but to his sisters as well. So yes, I questioned. I NEVER went in and said a grade needed to be changed. It was ALWAYS, "Can you explain this to me?" If I did not get an answer that made sense, I did go to Mr. Jack.

<u>Mr. Jack:</u> Now, it says right here, student's mother requested her son be placed in a self-contained English class as he received a 56 on the midterm exam. But this was a discussion though. It wasn't just the mom saying I need this, it has to happen, there was discussion about it and there was a placement change made at the meeting.

This next section sums up much of the district's mentality. All they are concerned about is that a student passes. Blake completed a project. He worked very hard on it and did a great job. He completed all the requirements and then some. He only received an 83. He was upset and went to talk to the teacher. The answer he got was, "You got a B. You should be happy with that." Blake got home, told me, and yes, I contacted Mr. Jack. There were no constructive comments from this teacher. There was no direction. There was no explanation as to why he did not get higher than an 83! Below is the testimony.

WATERS:

Q: The student was later upset to learn that he only received an 83 on the project.

A: Right.

Q: In your view is an 83 on a project a good grade?

A: Yes.

Q: For an IEP student what is your assessment of an 83 grade?

A: I would consider that mastery.

Q: I call your attention to the --

A: I should point out that 65 is passing.

There was also discussion about the Wilson Program. The District kept saying I continually rejected the offer every time it was made. This is actually true. However, again they refused to take any responsibility in the ridiculous scheduling they were offering. I also talked about this previously. One time they wanted him to drop ASL to make room in his schedule. Another time, they wanted to change his schedule halfway through the year. A third time, they gave me four days notice to start him in a summer program where he would have to go to a school for "Behavior Challenged" Students. A fourth time, they wanted him to drop TV Production, which, by the way, is what he wanted to study in college.

It was my understanding the District could not hold back services based on scheduling. Blake could have gone in early, stayed later, or had a private tutor at home. None of those options were offered.

When Blake was tested outside the district, one of the recommendations was to possibly attend a special school. I did, indeed, look into some of them. The ones closest had waiting lists that were almost two years long! A third program was much farther away and did not really have a large enough sports program.

This was another issue the attorneys took on. They could not believe I did not come to them for help to look into these schools. The fact that I did not have a discussion with them was definitely held against me. I told them I did my own research and it was not going to work out because of the wait time. The reality was that my decision saved the district money. They would have been required to pay for the school and the transportation since they could not accommodate my son.

WATERS:

Q: Was there a lengthy discussion on it or was there simply refusal on the part of Mrs. Mellon to consider it?

A: There was no further discussion once Mrs. Mellon said that. So there was not a lengthy discussion.

As part of Blake's IEP, sometimes he was offered a consultant teacher and sometimes he was offered resource room. There was always much discussion about the two because the services sometimes seemed to be nothing more than a glorified study hall.

WATERS:

Q: Were consultant teacher services offered at this meeting?

A: Yes, but that -- see, and I'm going to be honest, I don't necessarily fully always understand completely consultant teachers versus resource room.

Many of my meetings could last 2-3 hours. I always have an agenda prepared, but it usually is not the same as the person running the meeting. So, after all their business is done, I bring up my concerns. Typically my questions lead to more questions or clarifications. Mr. Jack agreed with me:

Waters: And why do you, why do these meetings last so long, let's speak about this one?

A: "Well, one reason is because Mrs. Mellon has a lot of questions and one of the questions that I really was almost positive happened at this meeting was about the role of the direct consultant teacher or the resource room teacher. And she really wanted clarification on exactly what that person is supposed to do. So because it's not just a matter of we're offering this, this is why, do you agree, its also well, let's discuss that. So with most points there was a long discussion. There were a couple of outside placements discussed. And we even brought up a couple of those, such as the Churchill School.

REGARDING BLAKE'S TEACHERS:

Q: As a matter of proper administration does the district generally allow parents to select their children's teachers?

A: As a practice absolutely not, no, we don't.

Q: Does Mrs. Mellon attempt to make suggestions or to indicate who should be Blake's teachers?

A: Yes.

I often had suggestions as to what teachers I thought would be good for Blake, based on their teaching styles and his Dyslexia. He did not always get whom we wanted. Only once, did I say I wanted a particular English teacher. Blake had her previously and he would not have to start over with someone new. This teacher understood the dyslexia and Blake was comfortable with her. I never selected teachers. I only made suggestions. There were also times where his teachers would make suggestions they thought were a good fit. I would pass this information on to his Guidance Counselor.

*Another topic was testing. Did the exam actually test for knowledge or was it testing to see if the student could take a test. One particular example was a word problem on a math test. Blake got the entire problem wrong. There were three individuals mentioned in the problem. One was Ed, one was Mary, and one was Maura. He simply got Mary and Maura mixed up. I felt this was unfair. I really felt that it was unfair to **all** the students. This type of example happened over and over again. Yes, I did want him to be able to re-take the exam. They told us NO.*

The attorneys kept repeating I was only concerned with Blake's grades. No, my concern was that he be treated fairly. His directions were supposed to be specific. His goals were supposed to be measurable. When this did not happen, I brought it to the attention of the powers that be, over and over again. I can't say enough wonderful things about Mr. Jack:

Q: Can you tell me why Mrs. Mellon is thanking you for meeting with her today and why she states that you are now officially the only administrator who cared enough to ask a lot of questions instead of trying the preach the district doctrine?

A: We had an extremely long meeting which I absolutely invited, I did not try to cut it short, in which she pretty much laid out the entire history of Blake's schooling for me, from elementary school on. She mentioned his dyslexia at the time and she went on and on about all, what that means exactly. I took the stance that please educate me because again I am not a special educator so tell me everything you possibly can about Blake so that I am aware of it. At the time I also did believe that it was still very early on in Blake's education [at this school] and in my history, 13 years in administration, actually this was 12 years at the time, that most kids where a parent is this concerned end up having discipline referrals because of frustration usually or because of other things that get in the way of their learning process. So I also really wanted to know everything so that I understood what to do in case I did get any discipline referrals at any time related to Blake because I believe that any consequences given for behavior should be done fairly, not just because the book says this is what you did, that's -- this is what you get. All right. So the more I understood Blake the better for me in operating in the future thinking truly at the time that I may really get some concerning Blake because my history is that most kids with this many phone calls and this much concern it ends up happening. Maybe not at the beginning of their career, but it does end up at some point happening.

Another bone of contention was the fact that tests hardly ever came home. If the student did not do well on an exam, you were sent a note home to sign. I wanted to see the actual tests. Our district does not do that.

Q: Thank you. And as to the second point made by Mrs. Mellon in that e-mail to you concerning taking tests home, can you tell me what that is about, please?

A: Yes, she was very clearly expressing that she is offended as a taxpayer that kids, students are not given their tests to take home to be reviewed or seen by the parents.

Q: And what is your, what is your reaction to that, what's your view of that?

A: As a practice our district doesn't give tests back to take home because they are recycled. Many of them come from test banks which are, which also are related to the textbook. They are coming from the same publisher as the textbook. And some of the test banks unfortunately are not very extensive, so a lot of questions get used year after year. As a practice teachers don't send them home. She really wants them sent home.

Q: Was the, did you make it clear to her that she could come in and look at the test --

A: Yes.

Q: -- if she wanted to?

A: Yes.

So basically, I would have to take time off from work, to go in, and see a test in order to review it. I understand the teachers wanting to recycle tests but they can be more creative about it, especially with all the technology today. When all there was were mimeograph and Xerox machines, we always brought tests home. As a parent, I feel there is no excuse why this cannot be done.

The next topic was about taking notes in class. Blake was having issues with taking notes. He would try and take notes and then, in the process, he would miss what was being said next. Sometimes, he would then be told he was not paying attention. I had asked for him to be able to get class notes, so he could be more attentive to what was being discussed. Finally some teachers did help with this. Others thought it was a form of cheating. I continually asked that one of the items on Blake's To Do list was to learn Note-Taking Skills. This is not something that is taught, at least not taught well, in our district. My focus was to just have Blake learn the material, in the best way for him.

There was talk of Biology, especially the Bio midterm review sessions. These sessions were mandatory for Blake's particular class.

<u>Mr. Jack:</u> The bio midterm was also setup to replicate to some extent the regents that they would take in June. So it would therefore be good preparation for that state assessment at the end of the year. When Blake went he found, according to Mrs. Mellon, she's saying 100 people that were there. But basically what she reported back was that there were kids sitting on radiators, et cetera. There weren't enough seats, that sort of thing.

Blake was sitting on a back counter, half in a sink. Because there were so many kids, they moved the session into a larger room. Though I do think they had to do something, Blake was already frustrated. To sit in a review session of over 100 kids was going to be counterproductive for him. He went to the new location and then left. He called and told me he was leaving. I supported him and told him he could review with his Bio tutor.

The district felt I had no qualifications to make a determination as to whether the review session would have been helpful! They felt he should have stayed and maybe he would have learned something. Based on my years of experience with Blake, as compared to the District's history, when it comes to him, yes, I absolutely felt I was a better judge of what would be helpful, at that moment.

Mr. Jack: I also feel that extra help is valuable because there is extra instruction that goes on and that even with 100 kids in the room it certainly is no way near optimal to have 100 kids in the room. He might have picked up on something helpful. Her point is that with that many kids how could he really learn, why would that have been effective. Extra help obviously wouldn't normally be 100 kids; extra help is usually three or four.

Q: In your view who is in a better position to judge the value of extra help, you or Mrs. Mellon?

CARTER: OBJECTION.

HO: Sustain the objection.

Mrs. Rock: On what basis?

HO: I don't think it's relevant to the discussion, nor do I think he would have any way of knowing whether Mrs. Mellon is more effective as an educator. I don't know what she did We haven't heard Miss Mellon's background, so how would we know what Mrs. Mellon was able to do.

Rock: Well, I think he does know her background because he dealt with her over the course of several years.

<u>HO:</u> I still don't think he knows her background. I mean I think you can ask him if he thinks he's an effective educator and can judge those things, but I don't think he can judge.

This goes on for pages, debating my qualifications. I wanted to include this so the readers can see how much time was wasted on things that were not important. The hearing was supposed to be about whether or not Blake received the support he was entitled to and how this was going to be accomplished. The School's attorneys purposely kept going off on tangents and in the process, wasting our time and money and the District's as well.

In our District, the schools have what is called a testing center. Often a TA (Teaching Assistant) staffs it. This is important because many of the students who use the Center have special needs. For the most part, a TA is not usually qualified to work with these students. There are definitely exceptions. The District was not happy that I would ask who was in the Center and what their qualifications were. The same is true for proctors of certain tests. I needed to be sure whoever was reading the exam to Blake knew his issues and knew how to answer his questions.

Though at face value, I will agree, this all does seem to be over the top. What I need the reader to understand is this only came about after 6+ years of continual problems: including issues with proctors not knowing what was on Blake's IEP. Unfortunately, the high school, especially Blake's sophomore and junior year, had to deal with the brunt of my frustration.

<u>Mr. Jack:</u> All right, without reading the whole e-mail, because this is another long one I wrote, the general idea here was that, was project review and re-grading is always a possibility. Any time a parent asks we will certainly look at any project to make sure it was done accurately. And I also was stressing that I feel that all projects have educational value because there was some question as to whether this particular project was actually valuable to Blake's learning.

Q: And the other theme which was testing accommodations, take a moment to look at that, that's in the last paragraph?

A: Oh, okay. I don't believe we've had much testimony on that. Okay, there was mention of course as had begun in a previous e-mail and previous conversation, also as well, that Blake was hesitant to go to the testing center, obviously because of things that occurred in the middle school as well as this thing that occurred period eight previously to this date.

Q: Do you as a general rule go into so much detail with a parent concerning testing accommodations?

A: No.

Q: And why did you do that in this case?

A: I feel that obviously Mrs. Mellon has specific pointed questions. Her specific questions deserve specific answers. Some of them are in writing, in e-mails, some of them have been over the phone. But if she asked a quick question she would probably get a quick answer. But since she has a lot of detail she wants to know, I feel I should get back to her with a lot of detail. But the part of your question was do I do this all the time, no because I don't have -- very few parents ask with as much detail as Mrs. Mellon and want information in as much detail.

I found this next question to Mr. Jack condescending and degrading. It shows the negative opinion of the attorneys toward Students with Special Needs. It refers to Blake and his projects. Blake never got anything less than an A on a project until 9th grade Bio.

Q: Mr. Jack, there is a statement to the effect that Blake has never gotten less than an A plus on any project ever, similar to this so for him this was failing. Was this, was this comment surprising to you with an IEP student?

With his question, he is insinuating that an IEP student is slow or stupid and should be happy with an 83 on their project. This is just another example of how we were treated. Mr. Jack's response:

A: Truly is that 83 is a good grade which I have said at other times. My reaction is that whether you have an IEP or not 83 is a good grade. It's not 95, it's a good grade. That all we're really trying to achieve of course is 65. Many kids will go way passed that and when they go way passed that that's something to be celebrated. That's my true opinion on it.

"That all we're really trying to achieve of course is 65." I will not apologize for the fact that my expectations for my children are much higher than that.

Another issue was how the students were tested. There was one example of a vocabulary section of a midterm. The word was "zenith" and there were 4 choices. This word was never on any vocabulary list given to students in elementary, middle or high school. Blake and many others got this question wrong. I complained. Why are they testing them on words they never learned?

<u>Mr. Jack:</u> Mrs. Sinto being the English teacher. And she said very clearly that in high school we do start getting words in English assessments that are words that students should be starting to use in high school and that they would have learned along the way through life. That they would have -- in other readings that they've had perhaps it would have been in there and it's something they should know. If not then they can use deductive reasoning to help answer the question.

Her view on the subject is how can somebody be tested on something that they are expected to have learned along the way. What if they didn't learn it along the way, therefore, it's an unfair question. And not just the question but maybe therefore the exam itself was unfair.

This is high school and along the way students start to gain vocabulary understanding that they wouldn't have necessarily had on word lists. All right, and that a student should by now be beginning to develop deductive reasoning skills.

Blake has excellent deductive reasoning skills, but he does not think like the" average" student. This is common for those with dyslexia. They are often very creative. He sees things differently and asks your "not so typical" questions.

The District was also not happy there were times when I did not approve of who they chose to be at a CSE meeting. I had every right to express my disappointment with who would participate in the "what is in Blake's best interest" discussion. It did not mean that they were not going to be at the meeting, but as a member of the CSE, I had a right to give my opinion.

I was chastised for that too. Blake's 9th grade math teacher was the one in question. She gave him handwritten tests. Yes, I complained. She did notebook checks that for most students are helpful. For Blake this was a nightmare because of his lack of organizational skills, at the time. He was not getting the much needed help and support that I felt he was entitled too. He was essentially penalized for his lack of organization. Yes, I had a right to complain that this particular teacher was part of his CSE, yet she was.

The following transcripts continue to show how the district only wanted to drag out this case and focus on issues that did not matter, specifically, again, how many emails I sent. If certain members of the district would have done their job, much of this could have been avoided. I think any one who will read this, will be appalled.

Regarding Blake's goals and then the hearing itself, you will clearly see at which point the hearing officer is annoyed and I feel started to take it out on us. Instead, she should have been angry with the school's attorneys.

<u>Carter:</u> Actually, if I may respond to that, we've had testimony already from the one teacher who was working on the reading goals for the child with dyslexia and the teacher testified that upon her first presentation of those goals and objectives to the student in March the student had already mastered those goals. I think it's clearly already been presented by the district in their own case that those goals were not appropriate. And here we have a kid with dyslexia sitting here not getting anything to address his reading disability.

<u>Rock:</u> That's exactly what Mr., excuse me, but with all due respect that's exactly what Mr. Jack is testifying to throughout the course of this discussion of e-mails. He's talking about how they are addressing, among other things, the reading goals. And that's why it's, just why it's important that these e-mails be discussed.

<u>Carter:</u> Okay, as we've already had in testimony the two reading goals on their first presentation to this student he had already known those single syllable or two syllable words and they've never worked

on those reading goals subsequent to that. And now we're just having testimony about the parent complaining about the inappropriate IEP, but the district is not focusing its case on what the issues are and that is whether or not this IEP addresses a student's needs. And they are trying to do an end-run around the requirements here by focusing this on the parents frustration rather than focusing it on here are the evaluations, here's the IEP we developed and this meets the child's needs, which is what this hearing is all about.

Rock: I would suggest, Madam Hearing Officer, that you allow the testimony to continue and you can be the judge of how much weight should be accorded to the e-mail testimony.

Carter: We've got two attorneys sitting on the other side of the table and I've been very patient all day today when we have very limited, I don't know if there were six questions that might have been focused on the issues in this hearing. And we got, we just have what I can only characterize as generation of fees on the other side of this table and not focusing and –

Rock: Can we please --

Carter: -- extremely --

HO: I'd like it not to get --

Carter: It is extremely detrimental to a family who's also bearing the cost of this. It's one thing for them to be, to be doing this to their own client, but they're doing it to mine and I'm going to ask that the hearing officer call an end to it.

Rock: I'm sure when you took this case that you told the Mellon's that there would be a hearing here and you must not have guaranteed to them how short or how long it would be.

Carter: I certainly did not guaranty to them that we would have lawyers like this on the other side of the table. And I'm going to ask that the hearing officer get this hearing focused back on the issues so that one day we can be done and Blake can get a FAPE (Free and Appropriate Public Education).

<u>HO:</u> I think that's for me to determine. And I'm going to take offense now because I think that is my role to determine whether or not in fact the district did offer a free appropriate public education for Blake And, as I said before, there are two things on the table here. Number one, this is not material that the district bombarded the parent with. This is, this is information that the parent sent to the district and wanted answers to. And as I stated before, an IEP isn't just the four, five or six or seven pages that are written down. An IEP is the entire process which goes into the development of the evaluation of, the implementation of and all of the staff that, you know, provides the services indicated. And although some of it, I agree with you, has been extremely redundant and I've asked on several occasions that it be shortened, both the questions be shortened and more relevant, and the answers. It is difficult when there is this much evidence on the table that people are expected to have committed to memory each instance and I do think it is relevant to the case that the district is trying to make as far as the implementation of their IEP. I'll decide whether or not it was effective or not effective. So I feel I have to give them the opportunity to present their case. And I'm going to ask them again to

questions. And in some way I had wished that

<u>Rock:</u> I'm doing so. I'm up to 202.

<u>HO:</u> --they had been grouped in some way to address certain issues. As I see it there are five or six issues that were discussed in all of these IEPs, the issue of placement, the issue of the grading, the issue of accommodations basically are the issues that were addressed. And it would have been nice if they had been more concise and, you know, how many dealt with, how many e-mails dealt with each of them and more, but that isn't the way they presented the case. So as a hearing officer I will try and, you know, work with them to the best of my ability to have them consolidate some of their questions and I think they have really out of 300 and how many --

<u>Rock:</u> 331.

There was continual discussion about ASL, which I covered, in an earlier chapter. Mr. Jack was very instrumental in solving this issue.

OUR ATTORNEY NOW WAS CROSS-EXAMINING MR. JACK:

Q: Now, what are Blake's disabilities?

A: Blake has dyslexia. That was not his official disability as far as -- no, it wasn't his classification for sure because --I'm sorry. I would clarify that I do believe that disabilities don't exist within a vacuum. So if a child has a disability in one area it can certainly impact upon other areas.

Q: And the district in the time that you're aware that Blake resided in the district and based on your familiarity with his school records had they ever identified that Blake had dyslexia?

A: This is my understanding, without having records in front of me, that term was not in the early records. That there was talk about reading needs, I believe, but I don't think the word dyslexia was in there.

Q: Sir, you're not aware of the district having identified his dyslexia?

A: Not at all. No, I am not aware that the district previous to coming to high school had already identified dyslexia.

The next set of testimony will show some of the blatant ways the school's attorneys tried to discredit me. Supposedly, there were some teachers that said I berated them, made them feel nervous, and attacked them verbally.

OUR ATTORNEY CARTER TO MR. JACK:

Q: You used the word berate. Did Mrs. Mellon berate someone?

A: I would not say she ever did berate, I'm sorry, that's such a charged word.

Q: Can you point to anything in all the e-mails of Mrs. Mellon that was an attack on any individual?

A: No. That I would call an attack, no.

Just the opposite, I was extremely verbal when he had great teachers. Blake had a math teacher, whom my older daughter, had as well. I did say that Blake was having trouble with his foreign accent and his handwriting. However, I adored this teacher. Though he was not a good match for Blake, he was efficient, organized, and pleasant. He was caring and concerned and very helpful with Blake's tutor.

Mr. Jack said of some of the teachers:

"It kind of feels as though she's looking for the mistakes, like let's find them and then as soon as I find them I'm going to point it out to the school."

I have a lot of respect for many of the teachers and administrators. I have told most of them this personally and in front of others. I have also written many positive letters and sent them to the district. Some were written as reference letters. There are, however, others I have no respect for at all. I don't have to look for mistakes, they pop up everywhere: flyers with wrong dates, sheets with incorrect info, typos all over the place, computer links not up to date or wrong. And yes, I do point these out because those involved should know.

Teachers are quick to point out Blake's mistakes, but if he would hand in papers, the way some of the flyers come home, he would fail.

The worst, was the English assignment with major misspelling and grammatical errors. I brought this to Mr. Jack's attention. I did not want to embarrass Blake's English teacher because it was an assignment given to the whole 10th grade. A copy of this is included in an earlier section.

The last main issue of the hearing was about placement and goals. The correct order should be needs, goals, and then placement. Placement was always talked about first and then goals.

Hearings - Day 4 (May 20th)

Continuing with Mr. Jack:

Now, again, I have to say this. Most, if not all, of Blake's teachers from last year were nontenured. Some of them were fairly new at their practice, so they may not have been as communicative as they should have been. Perhaps because they maybe didn't know enough to respond as quickly to certain things, or to contact the parent early enough, when there was a problem. Where she (the Biology Teacher) was saying I just can't handle it, the stress level, I just can't deal with it.

And that is my fault? She's a special education teacher. Maybe she is in the wrong profession.

There was major discussion over the years about Resource Room versus Consultant Teacher. Depending on whom I asked, I usually got very different answers. The district did not like that I kept asking for clarification.

Mr. Jack:

Q: And what type of questions were those?

A: Those questions were asked often, okay. They were, she really wanted a job description for the resource room teacher and/or consulting direct teacher, whatever we call that. It was about what is the point of Blake going to resource room, is he there to learn organizational skills and to get ready, organized for going home and getting his homework done or is it really a homework center. That's pretty much what the conversation was ongoing. So, therefore, she wanted very specifically clarification on what the resource room teacher is supposed to be doing.

Q: And you thought that these were not appropriate questions?

A: No, I actually thought they were appropriate questions.

See Mrs. Rock's (school attorney) very obnoxious comment:

<u>HO:</u> Do you have any comment on that that you'd like to put on the record?

Carter: Yes. We spent about 90 seconds searching the record and we're not going to waste anymore hearing time on it. And we'll just point it out in our closing briefs if there's inconsistencies in this witness' testimony.

<u>Rock:</u> Are you going to make speeches or are you going to ask questions?

<u>HO:</u> It was a comment for the record. I asked for a comment for the record.

On my relationship with Mr. Jack and others in the school:

<u>Rock:</u> Sir, for future reference and for opposing counsel's benefit all the questions I'm asking are about ninth and tenth grade, okay? And I'm asking you to characterize your relationship with Mrs. Mellon that's developed over the past year and a half, two years?

<u>Mr. Jack:</u> I actually have continually believed that Mrs. Mellon and I have a very trusting relationship. That I have given her all the time she's asked of me. And that I would do whatever I could in my limited knowledge and understanding of special ed to assist her in getting answers to all her questions. I have always respected her. I have heard comments made by others that I don't necessarily always agree with, that has nothing to do with my specific relationship with her.

Q: Has Miss Mellon ever been discourteous to you?

A: I would certainly say not, no.

Q: Has Miss Mellon ever expressed in any way recognition of your efforts on Blake's behalf?

A: Yes.

Q: And how has she expressed that?

A: She said various things such as you're the only administrator whose ever listened. The district's not paying you enough, various things like that she said. Some in e-mails, some in person.

Q: And has she also expressed appreciation of any of the district staff members working with Blake?

A: Yes.

*The one meeting our student advocate attended, turned rather ugly when Mr. Fuchs (Head of Spec Ed) told me I was being **abusive** by sending all these emails.*

Q: Did Mr. Fuchs ever refer to Mrs. Mellon as abusive?

A: I don't remember it being abusive or maybe just the word abuse. I just don't remember the exact word. It was a strong word. It was a strong word. He was saying that her volume of e-mails was a form of harassment or abuse. And I don't remember the exact word. When we say strong language it certainly wasn't like improper language, it was just a very, very strong term about Mrs. Mellon.

Q: And what occurred after those comments of Mr. Fuchs?

A: My memory is that Mrs. Mellon, and I might have it wrong, this is my memory, she slammed her book shut and told the advocate you need to take over now, I'm done, I have nothing more to say at this meeting.

The school's attorney gave the last and most egregious comment below. It was part of a discussion about my wanting to ban the Head of Special Ed (Mr. Fuchs) from any further meetings. I did not approve of the way he treated me, at the earlier June meeting, even with out Student Advocate present.

Q: Is it unusual, do you recall a certain e-mail where Mrs. Fuchs -- excuse me, strike that, where Mrs. Mellon requested that Mr. Fuchs be excluded from a CSE meeting?

A: Yes.

Q: And is it unusual --

A: By the way, I don't know if it was an e-mail or just a phone conversation but I definitely remember that statement.

Q: And is it unusual for a parent to seek to exclude a Director of Special Education from a special education meeting?

A: That's very unusual.

Q: I have no more questions at this time.

RECROSS-EXAMINATION BY OUR ATTORNEY:

Q: Is it unusual, sir, for Mr. Fuchs to call parents names at CSE meetings?

<u>Rock:</u> Objection. No testimony in evidence on that subject.

Q: Is it unusual for Mr. Fuchs to treat parents as he did --

<u>Rock:</u> Objection.

Q: -- at the June 2007 meeting as he treated Miss Mellon?

<u>Rock:</u> Objection.

Q: Or is that typical practice in the district for Mr. Fuchs --

<u>Rock:</u> Objection. That's a -When you did stop beating your wife.

<u>Me:</u> I need to have that comment stopped. It's not even something to joke about.

Mrs. Rock's comment referred to a statement made earlier in the hearing by Mr. Waters. He was obviously frustrated with the testimony:

<u>Rock</u>*:* Objection. The same objection. There is no such testimony. You're asking when something happened that didn't.

<u>Waters:</u> It's like when did you beat your wife.

Me: That's unacceptable.

I believe these comments clearly show the character of the School's attorneys. Quite frankly, it made me nauseous to be dealing with them.

Mrs. Rice (Spec Ed) was brought back in for re-direct. Except for a very basic reading program early on in elementary school, specific reading programs were never mentioned to us, at that level.

A: Yes. I mean there's, you know, at the elementary level there's a foundations program that is an offshoot of Wilson and there's Wilson available at -- but once again I would, you know, I think that someone other than myself that's in a better position to give you a full description of those programs and availability.

Q: Were there any discussions about providing Orton Gillingham for Blake?

A: No, there was not.

Q: Was there any discussion about providing Lindamood-Bell for Blake?

A: No, there was not.

Hearings - Day 5 (June 12th)

Day 5 started out with Mrs. House, Blake's Guidance Counselor. I am not going to spend much time on this for a few reasons.

1 - The GC really had no say in any decisions that needed to be made. She was at times very helpful in making up Blake's schedule.

2 - She was helpful as a sounding board. I never felt she really understood where Blake was coming from, or me for that matter. She definitely did tell me several times she thought I was too involved.

3 - I always appreciated her honesty, I just did not always agree with her.

4 - There were meetings she could not attend because she was either not informed, or not informed in enough time, to change her schedule. There were also meetings that went long so she had to leave. I do not fault her for that at all.

5 - Guidance Counselor's are definitely swamped with their caseload.

6 - I saw no productive reason why she was even called to the hearings.

Next in was Mrs. Lackey – The Assistant Superintendent of Pupil Services. This was the woman that gave me an incomplete written report on Blake's Wilson Assessment. The top 2/3 of the paper was blank and there was no name! But I should trust that it was his. She also felt I was too involved.

Mr. Waters: Can you compare the interactions in this case with Mrs. Mellon to your experiences through the many years you've been involved in terms of frequency and the nature of the contact?

A: The nature of Mrs. Mellon's contact and the frequency and the intensity of them far exceeds that of any other parent I've worked with when I look at the whole staff, the building level, central office.

Q: Can you quantify that, is it a little bit more, a lot more, X times as many?

A: It's the most of any parent I've ever dealt with and for a child who's not nearly as severely disabled as other children whose parents I've worked with to me that's, it makes it even more remarkable.

Mrs. Lackey did not like to have anyone question her years of experience. I question often and in-depth because we have been so misled in the past. No one seemed to want to recognize the past or have any accountability for it.

Mrs. Lackey: The level of detail that Mrs. Mellon wants paid to Blake's program is excessive and in my opinion intrusive and does not actually benefit the child. In my own opinion I think it enables him and actually will ultimately provide a disservice to him. Questions such as where will a test accommodation take place, who's going to do it. Here is who I want to have do it. Those are, that's a level of intrusiveness that I've never experienced with any other parent.

Q: Have you experienced that level of intrusiveness, as you call it, from Mrs. Mellon?

A: Yes.

Q: Often?

A: Very, every -- yes. Very often. Her e-mails are going to for more depth than I feel that is required and seem to have more of a finger pointing feeling to them rather than to really have some quality conversations about what Blake could be doing to become a better student.

HO: **I'm going to intercede here and ask that we move forward. I don't think there's anything to be gained from a personal attack on the parent** and I just think if we have the facts in evidence --

Waters: I have one more question.

HO: Okay, I'll let one more question go.

Q: Do you have an opinion on whether the level of involvement that Mrs. Mellon has displayed has affected Blake's ability to succeed in school?

Carter: Objection. Lack of foundation.

HO: I'm really going to -- I don't think anybody could know that, so I'm going to take Miss Lackey also off the hook on that one because I really think that's a subjective question that no one could begin to answer.

Waters: All right, that being the case I have no other questions – one more, if I may.

Q: Did you meet with me prior to your testimony here?

A: I did.

Q: Go ahead, no other questions.

REGARDING MY MOTIVES:

A: I think I understand the question. I think you're asking me if I had been made aware of a supposed time that he was supposed to get an accommodation that he didn't.

Q: Yes.

A: I don't believe I'm aware of that happening.

Q: Mrs. Mellon never brought it, brought to your attention that in a prior school year there had been issues of implementing accommodations during exams and she wanted to make sure it didn't happen again?

A: Yes, yes, she did bring that to my attention.

Q: So her communication with you about accommodations was because of a past, at least in a parent's perception, a past failure to provide those accommodations?

A: I don't know if that was her sole motivation for bringing it to my attention.

Q: But she indicated that was one of her motivations?

A: Correct.

MORE FROM MRS. LACKEY:

A: If you're asking me by the term consider was it formally discussed at a CSE meeting? I don't believe it was discussed at the one I chaired. I can't account for any other meeting.

Q: What other reading programs does the district have available for students such as Blake?

A: We make available to students the reading programs that they require.

Q: And what ones are available?

A: I don't have an inventory of our reading methodologies in the district. If there's something that a student requires we provide it.

Q: But as far as you know the only reading program that was made available for Blake was the Wilson?

A: That has been the focus of our conversations.

HEARINGS - DAY 6 (JUNE 23RD)

Ms. Abeles was Blake's English Teacher and one of his favorites. I felt so bad for her. She was obviously nervous and it was evident the district had "spoken" to her.

Earlier they had made references to Blake regarding his going to extra help. Here is a case where the teacher made all the difference.

A: Blake is a student who, his attitude completely changed second half of the year. He started to put forth more effort and I really saw a change in his attitude and his behavior towards wanting to do well in my class. He did come for extra help more so when we started the research paper, that was a goal of his and he came pretty much every day after school and sat with me for a half an hour to an hour. He really wanted to do well. So I just saw an overall change.

Q: Was he in a sense rededicating himself because he did poorly at midterm, is that your impression?

A: No, I just think that he just wanted to bring up his grade. I don't think it had anything to do with him doing poorly on the midterm. Because he scored average with the rest of my students. It just, I don't know, he just came back third quarter and was just determined. I don't know if it had anything to do with the research paper coming up because that is a major grade and can be hurtful to their averages.

Q: Are you saying that a grade in the 70's is average in your class?

A: For a midterm exam, yes.

Q: Any particular areas of English language arts that you're aware of that Blake struggles?

A: Vocabulary.

Q: Is that the only area?

A: That's where I see his biggest struggle and the mastery of the content. He does get the basic comprehension of what's going on but struggles with the higher thinking, the analysis but he does okay when guided.

Regarding Ms. Abeles' anxiety level, why did they need to speak with her for an hour?

Q: Miss Abeles, prior to testifying today did you speak with anyone about your testimony?

A: I just needed to know what was going to be happening with my anxiety. I just wanted to know what I was walking into.

Q: And who did you speak with?

A: I spoke with Mrs. Lackey and her attorney just to see what the environment would be to help ease my anxiety.

Q: And how long did you speak with Miss Lackey? How long did you meet with Miss Rock?

A: The same time, half an hour.

Q: Was it at the same time you were meeting with Miss Lackey?

A: Yes.

Q: And when was that?

A: Wednesday.

Q: Wednesday last week?

A: Yes. Half an hour.

Q: When you said the attorney did you mean Mr. Waters?

A: No.

Q: Miss – Ms. Rock: Rock.

A: Yes.

Previously it was also mentioned that Blake did not advocate for himself:

Q: And do you have a comment about the progress that he's made in your class?

A: Yes, I am very proud of the success and the progress that Blake has made from the beginning of the year to the end of the year. He's done a great job in advocating for himself and just changing his attitude and doing well. So I am very proud of his progress.

KAY - OUR STUDENT ADVOCATE WAS UP NEXT:

Regarding the one meeting she attended with me:

A: But the first ten minutes or 15 minutes even was spent in scolding Mrs. Mellon about her, I believe the word used was abusive use of e-mail to contact and communicate with the various people involved with Blake's educational programming. This went on for some time and essentially wasting time that was very valuable in terms of discussing the issues. It wasn't just a point made it was repeat --

Waters: Again, objection. The witness is going well beyond answering the question.

Rock: Move to strike the portion that's not responsive.

HO: I'm going to allow her to continue because I think she was brought here to describe her participation in the meeting and she was asked for her view on this.

Waters: But respectfully the rules require that she answer questions, not give narrative.

Carter: Which rule are you referring to?

Waters: I'm sorry?

Carter: Which rule are you scolding Miss Mellon about her e-mailing the district --

A: Right.

Q: -- is that correct?

A: That's correct.

Q: Now, who was expressing those views?

A: Mr. Fuchs.

Q: And what was his role at the meeting, do you recall?

A: He was directing the meeting, as I recall, although the CSE chair was also there referring to?

Waters: Rules of evidence.

Carter: Which are very liberally applied in a hearing.

Again regarding how Mr. Fuchs treated me during that June meeting:

Q: Now, you said the word abusive was used by Mr. Fuchs?

A: Uh-hum.

Q: Is that the word he used, that the parent was being abusive?

A: Yes, that's the specific word he used.

Q: What was the tone of his voice during that period of the meeting?

A: Very scolding, very condemning,

OUR STUDENT ADVOCATES OPINION OF BLAKE:

Q: And what was your impression of Blake?

A: That he was very bright, friendly, happy, well-adjusted, well centered child.

Q: And did you speak with Blake about his educational needs?

A: Yes.

Q: And did he express any opinions to you ***in regards to*** *(I just had to point that out!)* what he needed?

A: I think he was aware that he had difficulty with reading. Didn't like reading. Found it difficult to get through books. We talked about a book that he was reading at the time and that it was difficult for him to do it. I think he just expressed a great deal of frustration, support of his mother helping him to try to get a handle on this issue.

Q: Do you recall what he was reading at the time?

A: It was a, sports related.

REGARDING BLAKE'S GOALS:

Q: And do you believe that these goals appropriately were addressing Blake's needs in reading?

A: No, I do not.

Q: Now, with them in front of you can you specifically point to why you didn't believe they were appropriate?

A: An annual goal needs to be specific measurable, observable, moving a child to, by taking some base steps along to some accomplishment at the end of the year that would really, in this case, bring his reading competence closer to what it should be for a tenth grader. And these are extremely specific and limited in terms of whether that goal of making Blake, assisting Blake in becoming a competent reader at grade level by, you know, these kinds of steps.

A big part of my discouragement with these hearings was the total waste of time with the meaningless and worthless questions. They spent an inordinate amount of time asking our Advocate about how much she charged, asking the same type of questions over and over again and in a variety of ways, about her background. They also inquired about when we talked, what we talked about, and how often we talked. Why was it any of their business?

The hearings often got heated because of the inane questions.

A: The specific reason she said it was --

Q: I didn't ask that.

Carter: Perhaps before Mr. Waters interrupts a witness' answer he'll let the answer finish.

Waters: I didn't ask her what her --

Carter: She only said one word. How can he possibly know that she's not answering his question.

Waters: Read back the question please and the answer?

Carter: He's being rude and badgering the witness.

HO: I'm going to ask that we remain civil. Please read back the question? (Whereupon, the last question was read back.)

A: The correct reporting of what Mrs. Mellon said was this is not an option because she and I knew that the Churchill School had no openings for September or the summer.

HO: That's irrelevant.

A: So we did not consider it an option that would solve the problem of programming for Blake

Waters: I ask that the answer be stricken as not responsive.

Carter: That answer is responsive, that's exactly why she was pointing out. He asked if that was an accurate reflection of what was said and she says no, it's not accurate because of these other components of it not being an option.

HO: Okay, I guess Mrs. Mellon is going to be on the stand, on the witness stand I am assuming and I think that that's something that we can discuss with Mrs. Mellon as to what exactly she said. I think at this point it was, it's a question of, it's a statement in the, and it's, it's embellished. I mean I'll let it go in the record at this point, but at some point I may have to ask that it be stricken.

THE LAST PART OF THE DAY IS DR X:

We had to pay her travel and time expenses for the day.

Her current position:

Q: Where are you presently employed?

A: I'm currently employed at [a top] School of Medicine in New York City.

Q: Do you have a title there?

A: Yes, I am a clinical associate professor in medical -- it's so long. Clinical associate professor in medical psychology in psychiatry at the department of psychiatry at [a top NYC] Medical School. And I am also the director of child and adolescent neuropsychology for the department of psychiatry at [a top NYC] hospital.

DR. X'S DIAGNOSIS:

Q: Could you tell us what was your diagnosis of Blake's difficulties?

A: On the basis of our testing my, and review of his records and developmental history my conclusion was that Blake's profile met criteria for a dyslexic profile of learning.

Waters: I'm sorry, criteria for?

A: He was a dyslexic learner. That his profile was consistent with developmental dyslexia.

Q: Could you describe for us what is developmental dyslexia?

A: Developmental dyslexia is an inborn, not acquired, difficulty with learning. Specifically an inability to read and write at a level one would anticipate based on one's intellectual abilities, academic opportunities in the absence of hearing, vision or other sensory impairments.

More results from the Dr: More importantly in overall there showed me that Blake's capacity for learning falls in the average range using the full scale IQ score. But that there are relative unevenness in his profile with relative weakness in a working memory as well.

On the pseudo word decoding test which is a test of phonological decoding in which the student is asked to read nonsense words aloud as if they are real words in English. Blake's overall performance fell at the 23rd percentile and about a fourth grade, mid-fourth grade level grade equivalent. Blake struggled qualitatively when we looked at the pattern of errors with vowels. In particular were very weak in consonants but vowel combinations were very weak, as well as more irregular letter formations seen in some words.

Suggesting difficulties with phonological decoding. Blake also showed a significant weakness in his fund of sight words as seen in his performance on the word reading subtest. On the WIAT-II reading word reading subtest has the student read increasingly difficult real words in English to a certain criteria where they fail so many words in a row. Blake's performance on that fell at the eighth percentile and at a mid to late fifth grade level.

It was important to notice, indicated in the report that that score needed to be interpreted in light of behaviors observed of Blake while he was doing the reading comprehension questions. Blake referenced back to the text on virtually every question and had to reread significant portions of the text to answer, properly answer questions. Further qualitative analysis revealed Blake could often answer factual or literal comprehension questions, struggled a great deal to answer any question requiring inference, prediction, deduction or higher order reading comprehension. And he also struggled to define contextual vocabulary words within passages.

Q: Were there any other weaknesses that were identified by the WIATs?

A: Yes, Blake also demonstrated a significant weakness in his spelling skills, which were very commensurate with his single word reading skills and fell at the 19th percentile and again at a mid to late fifth grade level.

Q: Is his poor spelling consistent or not consistent with the dyslexia?

A: Many dyslexic readers are often seen to be very poor spellers as well. And qualitatively and quantitatively in that section Blake showed difficulties for his grade placement as a ninth grader. He produced a one paragraph essay which was not written as a letter. Most individuals in high school produce a multiple paragraph long essay. His essay was also quite significant for immaturity in word use, grammar formation and very significant for problems with spelling as well.

A: At the time of my testing in January 2007 Blake showed tremendous strength in his mathematical reasoning and mathematical computational skills that were much higher than his language arts.

Yes, Blake also showed very good abilities and he showed no problems in terms of his basic memory abilities. His, most of his skills fell silently within the average range.

His academic weaknesses were in the language arts.

Q: What specific areas?

A: In reading and writing including spelling. We also looked at Blake's reading vocabulary, the ability to read correctly single words. And his single word reading skills fell at the 8th percentile, suggesting that Blake possesses age appropriate language vocabulary for expression and understanding of what people are saying, but with regard to reading vocabulary he shows a significant weakness.

Q: Do you have an opinion as to why he shows a significant weakness with reading vocabulary while his language vocabulary is not a weakness?

A: Blake has a very specific difficulty in reading and not in language.

Q: Could he learn, could he add to his reading vocabulary by reading on his own?

A: Blake needs the tools to be a good reader to improve his reading vocabulary.

Q: But as --

A: On his own, no, I don't think Blake would improve his vocabulary. Blake acquires vocabulary experientially would be my best professional opinion. He is an intuitive and observant average intelligence boy who listens well, understands what people are saying to him and learns, you know, every day through school and outside of school experiences. And I believe it's through those means that Blake has learned the vocabulary he has. So based on the limited amount of information Blake provided me, no, I cannot tell you what he's thinking and feeling. What I can tell you is I believe Blake holds his cards very close to his chest.

On the basis of our, of the testing what I saw was a student struggling with the basic foundation skills required to become a proficient reader. Blake in particular showed a lack of mastery of basic phonological principles, both in terms of understanding, you know, being able to understand the process of word decoding for reading as well as understanding the process of hearing sounds and translating them into letters for the process of spelling. Right now, right then when I saw Blake his foundation had many, many cracks and the house upon which he was building his reading skills were also quite vulnerable at that point. I also recommended that due to, you know, his particular pattern of learning that he also, and his age, that this program of instruction also be offered individually to Blake and also to bring him up to, hopefully close the gap between him and his performances and his intelligence be done on an individual basis and individually.

The following is about one of Blake's so-called goals and one example of how ineffective the Hearing Officer was.

Q: Do you have an awareness based on that of the approximate grade level I'm not asking for 1.8 or 7.9, but the ballpark grade level of specific sight words?

A: Yes.

Waters: Objection. I don't understand the question. I don't know whether Dr. X does.

HO: I'm sorry, I was writing something down.

Q: Let me give you some words and ask you if you could tell us the approximate grade level of these words okay? Rat, park, Lord, rib?

A: I'm sorry, after rat, park?

Q: I'm sorry, I'm trying to talk to the computer and you. Rat, park, Lord, rib, rash, run, rot, rush, rag, rod.

Waters: I'm going to object unless the witness can testify that there is such a thing as a grade level that's assigned to those particular words.

HO: I'm sorry.

A: I'm sorry.

Q: Is there such a thing as a grade level that's assigned to those specific words that you were given?

A: Do you want me to answer the question? I don't know where we are at here.

HO: Hold on for one minute. I think you need to rephrase the question with regard to that because first of all it's ten words and they could be on ten different grade levels. I'm not going to give you my opinion. So we're asking the witness as an expert witness so I think you can ask her something similar to where would that word be expected to be read or by what age child would that be expected to be read. I don't think unless, you have a standardized assessment, you can assign a grade level to it.

<u>Waters:</u> Can we first establish that the witness is in a position to answer those kinds of questions?

<u>HO:</u> Well, we are assuming she is an expert witness.

<u>Waters:</u> Can you assign a grade level to a given word?

A: What I can tell you is there are books that have these words in them that you can get.

<u>HO:</u> Adult --

A: Adult word list that I can refer back to.

Q: Are there also patterns of, for example, consonant volume consonant that are --

A: Yes.

Q: -- generally assigned a particular --

<u>HO:</u> Yes, except there are always irregular words. Don't go there.

Q: We'll try some words okay? How about the word rat, R-A-T?

A: Rat?

Q: What grade level would normally a child be expected to be able to read this?

A: An average child?

Q: Yes.

A: Being taught phonics?

Q: Correct.

<u>HO</u>: Well, you can't make that assumption if he was taught phonics.

Q: Let's assume a general ed --

<u>Waters</u>: Objection, objection, please. Unless the witness can establish that the word rat in isolation has a grade level connotation then these questions are not that appropriate.

<u>HO</u>: I'm going to let her answer them from her expertise and years of studying various tests.

A: I believe in a word reading test you would find the word rat at a first or second grade level.

Q: What about park, P-A-R-K?

A: Second to third grade.

Q: Lord, L-O-R-D?

A: Again about third grade."

I could not believe I was hearing this! The words they gave Blake as his goals were 1ˢᵗ - 3rd grade words and they all seemed to be okay with this!

Q: Rib, R-I-B?

A: I'm sorry?

Q: Rib, R-I-B?

A: Rib? Second grade.

Q: Rash, R-A-S-H?

A: Third grade.

Q: Run, R-U-N?

A: First grade.

Q: Rot, R-O-T?

A: First to second grade.

Q: Rush, R-U-S-H?

A: Second to third grade.

Q: Rag, R-A-G?

A: First to second grade.

Q: Rod, R-O-D?

A: R-O-D?

Q: Yes.

A: Again, first to second grade. They're all consonant vowel consonant type words. Very regular words in the English language.

Q: What about ice, I-C-E?

A: About third grade.

Q: Local, L-O-C-A-L?

A: Third to fourth grade."

There were even more. Then their attorney had the nerve to ask:

Waters: May I ask what the relevance of this line of questioning is?

HO: He's questioning, hopefully he's going somewhere with it.

Waters: Hopefully he's going tell us.

Mr. Stein: It's relevant. I'll move on.

Waters: Well, if you're not going to tell us why it's relevant I will move that it be stricken.

Stein: I believe there was testimony that indicated that these words, it's page 335 of the record in fact on cross-examination by Mr. Carter, these words were words that were specifically part of Blake's goals in reading for his IEP.

Waters: And whose testimony said that?

Stein: I believe it was Mrs Gilley giving her opinion of Blake's 5th grade testing:

Q: During fifth grade he also was evaluated?

A: Yes.

Q: Do you recall the results of that evaluation?

A: Yes, at that time Blake was administered - readministered the WISC-III. His performances also revealed ongoing weaknesses and a great deal of scatter in his academic performance such that his math skills were very well developed in the superior range whereas his reading skills were in the low average range. And written language skills were in the low average range indicating ongoing language arts and learning disabilities.

Q: With respect to your diagnosis of developmental dyslexia is there anything that you see in the fifth grade evaluation that would be inconsistent with that, that diagnosis --

A: No.

Q: -- based on the fifth grade evaluation?

A: The fifth grade evaluation showed Blake to still show inconsistency and a lack of mastery of phonics, especially vowels. He also showed relative weaknesses in his verbal working memory at that time.

Q: Would it have been fair based on this evaluation, the fifth grade evaluation to have diagnosed him with developmental dyslexia at that point?

Waters: Objection. Objection. There's no foundation for that question.

Stein: It's in her psychological evaluation. She is a neuropsychologist.

Waters: It's in her review of others.

HO: This is a review that she did of others evaluations. I'd have to be prejudiced in giving my decision here. I think I'm going to allow her to answer it at this point.

Q: Do you need it read back?

A: My impression is that the data seen in the fifth grade testing is highly consistent with the data I saw when testing Blake in the ninth grade which I would therefore say is consistent with the diagnosis of dyslexia.

The District's attorneys then continued to ask a line of confusing and argumentative questions. They also wanted to focus on her fees. What we paid for the testing, her testimony and her time. Again, what did any of this have to do with Blake? They wanted to know if she discussed Blake's sports with us. **Then here comes the real shocker. They are accusing the Dr. X of looking at me!**

<u>Waters:</u> You keep looking at Mrs. Mellon, is that because she's telling you something?

A: No.

<u>Stein:</u> Objection. I'm going to object to the characterization that she keeps looking at.

A: I'm just looking at anyone.

<u>Waters:</u> Well, that is a fact, sir.

<u>Stein:</u> I think she's looking around the room. I don't think she's --

<u>HO:</u> Let's remain calm. Please, I know it's been a long day.

ABOUT BLAKE'S SPORTS:

Q: Upon your evaluation of Blake should his participation in sports be in any way at the expense of remedial reading instruction?

A: I believe instead of the word expense I always believe in balance.

Q: So he should have both?

A: I believe he needs both.

Q: If a choice has to be made whether at a given period he goes for remedial reading instruction or shows up an hour late to basketball do you have an opinion on whether or not which of those two choices he should accept?

A: Again, I would need to know if it's consistent. Is this all the time. I believe both are equally important for Blake.

Q: So it's your opinion then that basketball is as important as reading instruction?

A: I believe basketball plays an important life in Blake's development psychologically. I believe reading plays an important part in his life as well.

Q: And is it necessary for him to learn and progress?

A: Pardon me?

Q: Is sports necessary for him to learn and progress?

A: Depends on how one defines learning.

Q: All right, as you define learning?

A: Learning --

Stein: Object.

HO: I'm going to allow her to answer.

A: Learning can involve academic book instruction and learning also involves relationships with other people, our cultural society. Learning involves not only what you absorb through the actual academic process but also participation of being a person in a community as well.

Waters: For what it's worth I share that view.

HEARINGS - DAY 7 (AUGUST 12TH)

Since I was the one called for the day, I am not including any testimony since almost everything was covered in previous chapters.

HEARINGS - DAY 8 (AUGUST 27TH)

Again. I was on the stand all day. The attorneys spent most of the time going one by one through all the expenses we incurred. They went through each tutor asking me what it was for and what their qualifications were.

They tried to trip me up on who said what when. They were antagonistic and tried to make it seem like I had my own agenda instead of what was in the best interest of my son. Their tone was very condescending.

Hearings - Day 9 (October 7th: Final Day)

The entire transcript, for this last hearing, is included below. I am on the stand for the **third** day, and tensions are flaring. It's long, some of it is boring, some of it is absolutely unbelievable but I thought it was important to include for several reasons.

I wanted to expose the system. I wanted others to see how much of it had nothing to do with helping Blake. I wanted to show the absurdity of the process. At one point, the Hearing Officer talks about delays. We did need to delay two of the scheduled hearings due to a personal family issue. What the Hearing Officer does not mention is that a typical day didn't start until 9:30 or 10am, there was always an hour for lunch, and there were days when we ended at 3pm. Once I think we actually went to 4:30pm. It will also show you a typical day in a hearing. The following is a quick read. Unbelievable but true.

<u>HO</u>: Well, I feel for both, and for myself and Ms. Lackey as well, in that we have dedicated a lot of time, along with the Parent and the two attorneys, to the Hearing, extending it further. It has been going since what, last February, {*it is now October!*} I believe. Seems to be an extensive amount of time, and then we are going to probably have at least another two weeks for brief writing, and then ten days for me to write a decision. So another month ahead.

So the likelihood that anything is going to be established much before the end of November, beginning of December, is not going to be very likely anyway. Why don't we do the Recross Examination of the parent, and see how that goes, and what time frame we are, and you said you wanted to go through some of paperwork, which will probably take about how much time?

<u>Waters:</u> Half hour, I would think.

<u>HO:</u> You could count on an hour then.

<u>Waters:</u> They teach you that in law school, day one.

<u>HO:</u> We will see where we are at that point. Who is the witness that we are looking at? Is she a District employee?

<u>Waters:</u> Yes. Mrs. Cookie. She's the one that's most familiar with the transition services.

<u>HO:</u> If we wanted to bring her this afternoon, would she be available?

<u>Waters:</u> I don't know.

<u>Lackey:</u> She has other obligations today. I believe she has meetings already scheduled with parents for her job, and other duties that she's attending to.

<u>Waters:</u> For the record, I have not gone over the anticipated testimony with Ms. Cookie. I know Mrs. Rock has. I touched base with Mrs. Rock late yesterday. She's pretty sick, and she's not available, and although even if we could consider taking Mrs. Cookie from whatever else she has to do, which would in itself be a burden, we don't have Mrs. Rock here.

<u>HO:</u> Let me ask one more thing, because Ms. Rock isn't here, so even calendaring is going to be difficult.

<u>Waters:</u> What I would respectfully request is that both Carter and the Hearing Officer schedule with Ms. Rock does not—I'm not going to be available. Ms. Rock is going to have to do that and that was our plan.

<u>Carter:</u> This is an extremely limited issue, and if Ms. Cookie has more that fifteen minutes of testimony, I'm going to be surprised.

<u>Waters:</u> You want to withdraw your claim that the School District hasn't provided appropriate transition services? We could get that off the table.

<u>Carter:</u> No. But the District has the burden of proof, and had an

129

obligation to address this when they put on their case, and they never called Mrs. Cookie, and now you want to extend this, at great expense to the parent, because you know, I'm coming from upstate, and further delay to the process.

HO: Do you think it's possible that we get Ms. Cookie on the telephone?

Waters: That won't help me.

HO: Maybe we could get Ms. Rock on the phone, as well.

Waters: We're going to have her testimony over the phone?

HO: I have done it before. I mean, if we are saying it's not going to be extensive.

Waters: I object to that, and I would remind---

HO: At least Ms. Rock on the phone as soon as possible to schedule, because as I said, we are getting to the point where it's getting really out of hand with the extensions. I know on our last extension, the next extension is still –the compliance date, I think is 11-19.

Waters: I would remind you, although I'm sure you probably know that the last two extensions were at Parents' request, and I'm not suggesting that they were in any way unreasonable, but they are not the School District's fault.

It is the District's fault that we had so many days of hearings!

HO: I understand that did throw everything off considerably, because I know you have some obligations as well. Well, why don't we go ahead and do this, and then we will discuss at the end of the Recross Examination where we are for the day.

RECROSS BY MR. WATERS:

Q: Good Morning Mrs. Mellon. You testified in you Redirect testimony by Mr. Carter, that since fourth grade, your son is still testing at a fourth or fifth grade reading level. Do you remember that testimony?

A: Yes

Q: What do you mean by that?

A: When he was tested by Dr X, those were the results that I received from her, that he was still reading at fourth or fifth grade level.

Q: Are you finished? I don't want to interrupt your answer.

A: Yes.

Q: Is it now correct that Dr. X, in her report, stated that you son comprehended at an eighth grade level, in January of 2008?

A: I was talking about reading, not comprehension. You asked me about his reading level Reading and comprehension are two different things.

Q: What do you mean by reading then?

A: Actually taking a book and reading the words.

Q: In order to comprehend what you are reading?

A: It makes it difficult to comprehend, if you are reading incorrectly. But if somebody is reading to him, or he is reading along with somebody, then his comprehension is there.

Q: Then what, in your understanding, was Dr. X telling us when she reported in writing that Blake comprehended what he read at an eighth grade reading level, what did that mean?

A: That means he has the ability to understand what is being read, not necessarily that he could read it on his own and comprehend it.

Q: Is your understanding then that she was telling, or us, that he comprehends when something is read to him, but not when he reads it himself?

A: Correct.

Q: So your understanding is that Dr. X is not saying that Blake can comprehend when he reads at an eighth grade reading level?

A: When he reads on his own, without assistance.

Q: Yes?

A: That is my understanding.

Q: You also testified, Mrs. Mellon, that the district psychologist did not have a clear understanding of what Blake's needs were in February of 2006, when she did her evaluation. Is that a correct characterization of her testimony?

A: What needs are we talking about?

Q: I'm looking at your testimony.

A: Talking about Ms. Heart, with eighth grade testing?

Q: Let me find it. Maybe it will help. (Pause)

Q: I an answer to one of Mr. Carter's questions, I'm reading a statement in the psychologist's report that this particular school psychologist did not have a clear understanding of what Blake's programs were or are because he is not reading anywhere near grade level. Not that's what the transcript says you said. What did you mean by that?

A: Well, first of all, she made some drastic mistakes on the testing that she did, that she admitted, and he was not reading up to grade level.

Q: Now, Mrs. Heart in that report recommends that Blake continue classification of learning disability. What, if anything, does classification for learning disability mean to you, in terms of the child's special education needs?

A: Well, I was trying to get clarification from the as to exactly what the learning disability was and how they were going to address it, because they just seem to lump it into a learning disability.

Q: What is a learning disability, under the federal and state regulation, as you understand it?

A: I'm not the expert, and I'm just - all I know is about my son, that he has trouble reading, and he has trouble with vocabulary, and all of these things that you are questioning me on, I'm not the expert. It's the thing that the school psychologist was supposed to be doing. He wasn't getting better. He was going through the motions. He was failing classes. Hence, we went to the additional testing which you all know, and now he got the result from that. So I'm not the expert in what that is.

Q: Tell us what classes he did, in fact, fail?

A: We already went through that once before.

Q: Yes, we did.

A: I don't have these notes in front of me now, but I know he definitely failed ninth grade intensive English for the first half of the year, which is why they moved him to self contained. He definitely failed regular Global in ninth grade, which is why they moved him to the self contained just for some exams.

Q: You testified in your Recross that at the June CSE meeting, that the District did not have any representatives of a private school. Do you recall having given that testimony?

A: I believe somebody asked me if they were available, and I said they didn't bring it up, so I don't thing they were available.

Q: Did you bring it up?

A: It was brought up, and I said there was no need to talk about it because I had already researched that, and there were no openings available for that September. I had gone to a conference for the International Dyslexic Association, that March. They had a whole room of a lot of these schools that were within the area, that was even confirmed by my student advocate, that said there is no openings, a waiting list of a year or two or three to get into some of these schools.

Q: I'd like to make it clear that at no time did you ask the School District to sent out any packet to any private school, is that correct?

A: That's correct. There was no need to. There was no availability in those schools.

Q: You testified in your Recross Examiniation that prior to Dr. X's report, that you were not aware that Blake was reading on a fourth or fifth grade level. Is that a correct characterization of you testimony?

A: I just know he wasn't reading up to level. I didn't know what specific level he was at.

Q: Were aware that Blake had any learning disabilities, prior to Dr. X's report?

A: Yes

Q: When did you first become aware that Blake had a learning disability?

A: First grade.

Q: When was he first classified?

A: Second grade.

Q: What was the nature of his classification in second grade?

A: Learning disabled. I was told when there was a difference of two years between English and Math scores, they are automatically considered learning disabled.

Q: It's correct then that both you and the District acknowledged that Blake had a learning disability, relatively early on in his education?

A: Correct.

Q: What you disagreed about, ultimately, as the nature of that disability, is that correct statement?

A: That's part of it.

Q: You testified in your Recross that you sent an email to the District on February 27, 2007, that, quote, Blake is competently reading and comprehending on his own, somewhere between fourth and fifth grade level, and it is testament as to how bright he is that he has successfully – I use that term loosely, I'm just quoting what you said-make it to school, to this point?

A: Yes.

Q: Did Dr. X, in her evaluation, do any testing of Blake's IQ?

A: I believe she did.

Q: Do you know what her result was?

A: I believe he tested average IQ.

Q: Is it your testimony that that is not true?

A: No. It's my testimony that he has developed some compensatory skills to go along that.

Q: It's not because is IQ is significantly above the average level?

A: No. But I think you could determine what being bright means in several different ways. It doesn't mean your IQ.

Q: How do you measure how bright a person is?

A: I think there is all different levels. Like I said, he's had to develop some wonderful compensatory skill to get him that far.

Q: Is there any doubt in your mind the Dr. X's score, is accurate?

A: I believe it was accurate at the time when he was being tested. I do think-I do know if people are tested on different days and different time, there might be some fluctuation. But within the realm of a certain scale, it seems to be pretty consistent. I believe his IQ has tested higher on the second grade testing.

Q: But you are not suggesting that Dr. X's testing was not correct?

A: No

Q: Do you know what the Wyatt examination is, Wyatt 2, specifically?

A: I know it was one of the tests that they tested him on.

Q: All right. Do you no whether the Wyatt tests reading comprehension?

A: No, not off the top of my head. I'd have to look at the tests.

Q: do you take issue with Dr. X's finding that Blake's reading comprehension, in terms of overall performance, fell in the average range, the 45th percentile?

A: If that's what she has.

Q: What information did you have, from any source that Blake has been able to succeed in school up until January of 2007 because he is so bright, what information did you have that underlies that?

A: That's the consistent feedback I have gotten from any of his resource teachers.

Q Would you tell us who, and when, please?

A: I'm sorry. I'm just getting really frustrated with this. I feel like I'm on trial, and this has nothing to do with the issues of my son. I'm sorry.

HO: I'd like you to counsel you Witness. I know this is a hard time for you.

Waters: Apparently, Mrs. Mellon doesn't fully appreciate the fact that it's my job to Cross Examine.

A: You are going to go back and talk to every single resource teacher? That would have been done already. I could give you Mrs. Bear, Mr. Carlos. I could give you Ms. Salve.

Q: Did either of those people issue any written report you are relying on?

A: I'd have to go back and check the progress reports.

Q: Do you know what the requirements are for a Regents diploma for a child who attends public high school?

A: I believe so.

Q: What are the requirement, Regents requirements, for Blake?

A: Regarding what specifically?

Q: In order to get a Regents diploma, what do you need to do?

A: A certain amount of courses he needs to pass the Regents, because he's classified, he has to pass them with over 55.

Q: Do you know what Regents he is required to take?

A: Yes

Q: Do you know what Regents he took?

A: Yes.

Q: Tell us please.

A: He took a math A Regents. He took a Biology Regents. He took an Earth Science Regents. I think that might be - and a Global Regents.

Q: English Language Arts?

A: No

Q: Did he pass all of his Regents?

A: Yes, and he had a lot of tutoring in order to do that.

Waters: I ask a question and I'm entitled to an answer, not other that that.

HO: I think we can ask that the second part of the comment be stricken from the record, as not unresponsive to the question.

Q: Mrs. Mellon, what is your understanding of the requirement of any school district, in terms of it's obligation to educate a child with a disability?

Carter: Objection. The party's understanding of the law isn't an issue that the Hearing Officer is going to be ruling on, and it's not relevant to whether or not the District is providing the student-

HO: You may be heard, but why don't you just rephrase the question to make it more specific.

Q: Under the IDEA, is the School District to provide everything that a loving parent thinks that her child should have, in terms of advantage?

Carter: Objection, calls for a legal conclusion.

Waters: May I be heard on that?

HO: Yes

Waters: The record is replete with Mrs. Mellon's efforts, for lack of a better word, to mold her son's education, to decide who teaches what subject, to decide what class he should attend.

Carter: Perhaps Mr. Waters wants to cut right to closing arguments.

Waters: I am asking a question.

HO: I'm going to ask you just to be more specific. If you are asking for an opinion, ask for an opinion. If you are asking for a statement of fact---

Waters: I have.

HO: It was interpreted by Mr. Carter as a statement of fact which he doesn't think his client has the professional acumen to answer, at this point.

Waters: With due respect, that's the heart of this case.

HO: Let's repeat the question please.

(The previous question was read back)

Waters: In your opinion.

Me: Would you like a yes or no answer, or would you like my full answer to that question?

Waters: We could accept both.

A: The first part of that is, no. I don't expect them to do everything. However, I do expect them to step up to the plate when they have missed something that should have been handled and handled years ago.

Q: Does the IDEA require a school district to accede to a demand that a child's teacher be changed?

A: I don't know how to answer that question. I have never demanded a teacher changed.

Q: Did you request that a teacher be changed?

A: I have asked for opinions on whether or not the teach should be changed.

Q: Did you ever request that your son's schedule be changed?

A: Again, I have asked for opinions on whether or not they thought this was appropriate for him.

Q: If the School District - withdrawn. So when the School District rendered an opinion that indicated that Blake was being successful in any given class, you respected that recommendation and didn't ask for any change?

Carter: I'm going to offer an objection. This whole line of questioning was covered on the first Cross Examination Mr. Waters conducted, and we are only now rehashing things, after Mr. Waters has had a chance to read the transcripts from the first Examination, and now he is going through the same questions again to create a redundant and overburdensome record.

HO: I have very liberally allowed both attorneys, I think, to go well beyond the scope of some of the issues, mainly to ensure that I'm not challenged on trying to constrain either attorney from getting their case on the table, so to speak.

I'm going to allow Mr. Waters one, or two, three more question in this area, but I do agree. I don't want to burden a more burdensome transcript that we need. So we should really just focus on what the Redirect was at the particular point in time.

Waters: If we could read back the last question and have it answered, I will let it go at that.

(The previous question was read back)

A: You'd have to give me more specifics, because I'm not sure what you are talking about.

Waters: All right. In view of the limitation to the Recross, I have no other questions.

HO: Okay.

Waters: What are we doing now?

HO: Are we going back again?

Waters: We have had Direct, Cross, Redirect, Recross. Now we are having a Reredirect?

Carter: The issue on this comprehension issue that was not brought up before, and now it's been brought up on Recross.

Waters: I will site you the page of the transcript.

Carter: The means by which you brought it up here were not covered in prior testimony.

HO: My mind isn't good enough right now, after six weeks of a delay, to tell you whether or not it was or wasn't. If you want to take a break, both of you could go through the transcript.

Waters: I don't need to.

Carter: I have mine. I believe I could cover this in about three questions.

HO: The question is then, we will have to go back to Rerecross, and I don't know if it's appropriate. I have never done that. So at this point, I don't know what issue he is citing, so why don't we give Mr. Waters the time to – do you want to cite where it was brought up?

Waters: Sure.

Carter: Are we doing a couple of minutes break here?

Waters: Give me a break, and I will find it. (Pause) Okay.

HO: There been an objection on the part of Mr. Waters for Mr. Carter to go back and do a Reredirect, based on the claim that he raised new issues which really should have been brought up during the Recross. But anyway, Mr. Waters will now state where it was done in the Redirect.

Waters: Sure. On Page 1424, Mrs. Mellon gave testimony as to Blake's reading level. On Page 1432, she gave testimony as to her opinion that the psychologist who tested Blake in 2006 did not have a clear understanding of what Blake's need were. On Page 1332, Mrs. Mellon testified incorrectly that the Heart report made no recommendation for reading. On Page 1442, she testified that the School District did not have any representatives of a private school at the meeting.

Carter: if I may interrupt, my limited Reredirect of the parent would be specific to the issue of the reading comprehension that Mr. Waters raised this morning. Is there anything there on the reading comprehension?

HO: I think we have documentation within the record of what the report says and doesn't say. At this point, I don't know.

Waters: Dr. X's report is the cornerstone of the contention with respect to the child's evaluation, and that's a matter of record.

HO: I don't know what's going to be gained from having the parent go back and do this again and again.

Carter: I'm going to call Mrs. Cookie next.

Waters: As I have explained to Mr. Carter, Mrs. Cookie is not available now and she has never been identified by Mr. Carter as one of his witnesses. His purpose in calling her this morning as his witness is simply a ploy, because he told me yesterday that he might have one other parent witness, besides, Mrs. Mellon, available this morning, and there is only Mrs. Mellon available. At no time did Mr. Carter indicate to me that he wanted to call Mrs. Cookie as his witness. If he want to do that, he is certainly - I will permit him to do that at a subsequent hearing, when she could be available.

HO: She was given no notice?

Waters: She's not on his list.

Carter: Mr. Waters was informed yesterday by me, in a phone call, that Mrs. Mellon was going to finish her examination, and that I had one other witness perhaps, from Huntington, which I did not anticipate to be here today, and Mr. Waters did not inform me that he was going to be asking for additional days, and that we are going to drive down her for about a half hour's worth or work. If Mrs. Cookie is working today----

<u>HO:</u> Gentlemen, I think, as I said before, I think both of you were equally liable for – we could have finished if we had known this. We could have finished the Recross Examination in a half hour on the last hearing date, but we didn't, because we knew that you were still anticipating another witness, and I think there was another rebuttal witness that Mr. Carter had been thinking about, and there have been several delays, and I will give Mr. Carter that have certainly not been at the District's wishes, and I'm certainly sure they weren't at the Parents' wishes either. But they were just life experience kinds of things, and life happening kinds of things, that created the need to delay the hearing. I'm not happy, as I said, and I feel badly for the District expense, as well as Mr. Carter, because it certainly incurs quite a large expense for them, my bill, and the Stenographer's bill, and everything, so that I'm not happy about doing it. But I'm going to give Mr. Carter – give the opportunity to go forward with the Rebuttal.

<u>Waters:</u> Are if you have another witness, are you bringing someone forward?

<u>Carter:</u> I'm Calling Mrs. Cookie.

<u>HO:</u> She's not available. She's been given no notice.

<u>Carter:</u> She's working today, and we could have her subpoenaed to be over here right now, or I don't mind waiting around seeing as we are already here.

<u>HO:</u> We have been told by Mrs. Lackey that she has prior commitments. Since she was given no notice, I don't see any reason to disrupt her day, and a day with other parents that may be have taken time off of work and other.

<u>Carter:</u> I can't believe that we are going to have a half hour of on the record stuff.

<u>HO:</u> I can't believe that we have delayed this case as many times as we have.

If the District's attorneys could have worked full days…

142

Carter: Perhaps the District can be caused to rest it's case now, rather than deal with rebuttal witnesses.

Waters: I will rest my case, if Mr. Carter will redact or eliminate that portion of his complaint that alleges that the District didn't provide appropriate and proper transition services.

Carter: The IEP speaks for itself, and there are no transition services on the IEP.

HO: As I said, I'm going to allow the District one more day of hearing. It could be half day, if that's all we need.

Waters: I don't see it going beyond another half day, and I'm very sorry.

Carter: I'm not available till after November 10.

Waters: We could be available on many days before that, but I think in all fairness, we ought to check what days Ms. Rock is available.

HO: I got a disturbing email - in fact, I think I'm going to ask the parent to step out of the room, if you don't mind, and go off the record. (Discussion held off the record)

Carter: I did have tomorrow's hearing canceled, so I could do tomorrow.

HO: Tomorrow is Yom Kippur Eve, and I'm expecting guests. If we could it tomorrow morning, I don't know if you are available.

Waters: I will make an effort to find out.

HO: I would come for the morning, but I'd like to be out of here the latest at two, three o'clock. As I said, I have ten people arriving for dinner, as well, and I have nothing cooked because I thought I had tomorrow to do it. But I will go home and cook today.

Waters: Are you working tomorrow?

Lackey: Yes, Partial day. I have another commitment in the morning, which is essential.

Waters: I will try and get Ms. Rock on the phone.

143

HO: And Ms Cookie, Are you going to have another witness or—

Carter: I'm calling Ms. Cookie.

HO: Ms. Cookie is being called by both parties?

Waters: He could call her first, if that's his pleasure.

HO: You are not calling the Huntington witness?

Carter: No.

Waters: Do we correctly conclude then that subject to the testimony of Mrs. Cookie as a parent witness, the parent has no other witnesses?

HO: That's what I have just asked.

Carter: Right.

Waters: Shall we recess for ten or fifteen minutes?

HO: I'm going to ask the parent to leave the room and go off the record for one minute. (Discussion held off the record.) Back on the record. What's the story?

Waters: Pursuant to your instructions, I spoke to Mrs. Rock. I had hoped that she'd be available tomorrow morning, but she has a court appearance that she has to make tomorrow. She can be available for sure on October 17, Friday. She could be available on October 14, which was Tuesday, which is next Tuesday, a week for today. That will be difficult for Mrs. Lackey, but she'll make that adjustment, if need be.

Lackey: I have an out of town training that morning. But if I'm the only person in the room, that can't make it—

HO: We could send someone. But you are not available?

Carter: Either of those days, I have hearings scheduled. I'm in Florida at a conference that evening.

Waters: May I respectfully suggest that you resolve this in a conference call, yourself, Mr. Carter, and Ms. Rock?

HO: Can we get her on a speaker phone to do it now? You are not available you said until –

Carter: November 11, unless I have something to clear off.

Waters: You want to try and get Mrs. Rock on the speaker phone?

Lackey: November 11 is Veteran's Day.

HO: That's why you have it open. What the next date?

Carter: After that I am pretty open.

HO: That's going to put us well into December, because even if we do it on the 12th, we won't get the brief probably until, optimistically, at the 24th - it will only be a half day probably - and then two weeks for writing briefs, that taken me into Christmas.

Waters: Well, is it possible that some of you dates will cancel or any of them will cancel?

Carter: I never really know and doesn't seem like things are settling, like that did in the old days.

HO: Everything down here is settling. I don't know what you are doing up there.

Waters: I don't know what to day that we haven't already said. If Mr. Carter is simply not available, there is not much point in bothering Mrs. Rock, who is not feeling well anyway. But I know that future scheduling on this is going to be –

Carter: Does she have a court appearance in the morning? Maybe in the afternoon.

Lackey: I won't be around tomorrow.

HO: I have to be out relatively early, too.

Waters: Jewish holy day.

HO: I don't know what to say. Are you both convinced this is an absolute must on the witness?

Waters: We have that issue out there. Mr. Carter believes that his client's interests are not served by taking it off the table, and that being said, we need to develop it.

Carter: The issue, Mr. Waters, is that you didn't address it in your Direct case.

Waters: That's certainly true.

Carter: You are trying to continue your case through rebuttal, when you had an opportunity to develop it on Direct.

Waters: The fact that you haven't addressed testimony to it—

Carter: What exactly are you rebutting in the parent's testimony?

Waters: I'm rebutting the allegation that the District hasn't provided transition services. It's in your Complaint. You haven't rested until this moment.

Carter: What I'm saying is rebuttal is to rebut some evidence put on by the Parent. What offer of proof do you have about what you are rebutting?

Waters: Simply the allegation.

Carter: The allegation was there when you made your Direct case.

Waters: My Direct case is a different thing. It's to demonstrate that the District has offered a free and appropriate education.

Carter: And the allegation about the transition plan was in the original Complaint, and you didn't address it in your Direct case, and now you are saying that the parent raised something on her case that you want to rebut, and I don't believe that there is anything in the Parents' case about that issue to be rebutted.

Waters: There is a lot of email stuff, and there was a disclosure that was sent to you by Mrs. Rock. You haven't had it five days. She tells me she sent it. I didn't.

Carter: I don't' remember seeing this either. When did she send it?

Waters: Probably Friday. If we had gone today, you could have objected to it. But I haven't seen it. I don't know what it is.

Carter: I don't believe I got anything from her. Did she perhaps mail to Buffalo?

Waters: It's possible. I don't know. That's a likely circumstance, if you haven't seen it.

HO: Well, this is what I'm going to do. I'm going to establish the 12th as a hearing date.

Lackey: 12th of what?

HO: November. That is the first time Mr. Carter says he is available, and I guess Mrs. Rock will be there.

Waters: With that kind of notice, she'll have to make herself available.

HO: I'm assuming she'll – I could set it earlier, and you are going to be thrown off your schedule. But you know, if your client objects to taking it out that far, I'm not happy with taking out that far either, quite frankly, because it does take me well into my December schedule. I don't care about writing the opinion. I could write it, but it's going to hit right I'm going to have a house full of company.

Waters: Are you available?

HO: I'm available pretty much any time –

Waters: May I –

HO: - for the next two weeks.

Waters: May I suggest that you and Mrs. Rock speak over the telephone. If you could find a date that she could live with, and Mrs. Lackey is available, we should get this done as soon as we can.

Carter: May I have a moment with my client? (Discussion held off the record) In the interest of getting the hearing completed, we are going to turn to hearing request paragraph five, which is the transition plan paragraph. WE are going to withdraw that claim, so that we could wrap this up today.

Waters: Okay.

HO: Thank you very much for agreeing to do that.

Carter: Just a caveat, that we are withdrawing it- it's an issue of the '07-'08 IEP, and we are withdrawing it for those purposes.

<u>Waters:</u> For purposes of this hearing?

<u>Carter:</u> for purposes of this hearing, yes.

<u>HO:</u> Are you suggesting that this may become an issue of a new hearing request?

<u>Carter:</u> What I'm saying is that our hearing request is limited to what we raised in the hearing.

<u>HO:</u> '07 – '08

<u>Carter:</u> And what was available at the time. So what I guess what I'm really saying is, I don't want the School District to be discouraged from providing an appropriate transition plan, as we move forward.

<u>Lackey:</u> We would do that.

<u>Waters:</u> Well, then we are finished.

<u>HO:</u> All right. Is that the agreement then? We have concluded this hearing. Both parties are –

<u>Carter:</u> May we have a couple of moments with the record issues?

<u>HO:</u> You should have the record by the 17th. The latest, I would say, the 20th.

<u>Carter:</u> Why don't we say the 20th?

<u>Waters:</u> Brief by?

<u>HO:</u> Two weeks is enough.

<u>Carter:</u> Good for me.

<u>Waters:</u> It's going to be to be good with Mrs. Rock, too.

<u>HO:</u> It's the 3rd.

<u>Carter:</u> Is the 3rd a Friday?

<u>Waters:</u> November 3rd is a Monday. Brief by November 3rd, okay?

<u>Carter:</u> Emailed and mailed that day?

<u>HO:</u> I will tan an email copy. But if you mail it now, I have a stipulation that I do because I don't have access to a law library, and

that's that any cases that are used in the brief, that I get a copy of as well. So that means probably I won't get them till the 5th.

<u>Waters:</u> You don't need the SRO decisions?

<u>HO:</u> You could just list those. But I want copies of any cases that are stated.

<u>Waters:</u> I do that, too.

<u>HO:</u> So I don't have to waste a tremendous amount of time trying to search them out. Then I'm going to say the date of receipt, which I'm assuming won't be officially till the 5th, because I will have to wait for the mail.

<u>Waters:</u> Should be mailed by the 3rd, the latest.

<u>HO:</u> So I'm going to say I'm going to receive it by the 5th, I guess. I will have until the 19th.

<u>Waters:</u> Fourteen days.

<u>HO:</u> So that's the 18th.

<u>Waters:</u> Decision?

<u>Carter:</u> the 5th is Monday.

<u>HO:</u> The 5th is Wednesday.

<u>Waters:</u> So the decision will be due on what day?

<u>HO:</u> The 18th or 19th, according to when I receive this stuff.

<u>Waters:</u> Why don't we make it the 19th?

<u>Carter:</u> Sounds good.

<u>HO:</u> Off the record.

13

PART 3:
WE LOST

After 9 days of hearings, no one heard a word we said. The whole process was futile. I was basically accused of being the problem. With all the hard evidence we provided and the witness testimonies, the district just brushed us aside. There was not a shred of accountability on their part. Basically, their claim was that the district did everything it was supposed to do because Blake passed all his classes. Nothing else mattered.

For those interested in reading the entire decision, I will post it at the end of the book under Addendum A.

POST-HEARING MEMORANDUM OF LAW IN SUPPORT OF A **DENIAL** OF ALL OF THE PARENTS' CLAIMS

14

BLAKE'S JUNIOR YEAR

By the time Blake started 11th grade, we had been through **eight of the nine days** of hearings. The atmosphere was tense because most of his teachers knew what had been going on, really did not want to get involved and they did not know who or what to believe. At least, it seemed this way, at first.

I was very upfront with them and explained I was just doing what was in Blake's best interest. If they had any concerns to please let me know. I also made it clear no matter what happened with the hearings, I had irrefutable proof of all my accusations and concerns.

His schedule seemed to be okay and the year started out as it always did, with high expectations this year would be different. Fortunately, we did have some high points, but there were low ones too. Blake was never able to catch a break.

At the end of September, Blake's Dad went into the hospital for emergency surgery. What was supposed to be a simple procedure turned into a nightmare. Due to many complications, his Dad was in the hospital for almost a month. He then had to be home on IV antibiotics for about six weeks. Of course, this was going to have an effect on Blake.

His schoolwork suffered and there was nothing anyone could do about it. It was just one more thing to deal with it and try to make sense of. There were tons of emails between the teachers and myself. We were desperately trying to get Blake back on track. There were ACTs to take, tutoring sessions to go to, and then the last straw…Blake did not make the Varsity Basketball team.

Since then, there have been some changes in the school's basketball program. When Blake was in 11th grade, if you did not make Varsity, at least in Basketball, your high school sports career was over. It was definitely the "unspoken" rule. He was devastated to put it mildly. Basketball is what kept Blake going. When he was busy, he always seemed to get more things done and do them well.

Blake muddled through US History/Govt, English 11, Chemistry, Health, and Broadcast Journalism. His grades ranged from a C to an A-. He failed his Chemistry Regents and barely passed his US History with a 68. What Blake did not know at the time, was if a student was "classified", all they had to do was get a 55 on the regents to get regents credit. I never understood that.

Blake's Chemistry teacher was an older gentleman that came from the business world and decided he wanted to teach. This was a teacher who truly wanted his students to learn. He had a policy about his tests. If you did not like your grade, you could re-take the exam. But in order to re-take, you had to come to a review session. You can re-take the tests as many times as you wanted.

This was one of the few times I would get frustrated with Blake. He did not take advantage of this opportunity as much as he could have. He didn't see the point and you could not explain the importance in anyway that would make sense to him.

Math…I talked about some of this earlier but it is so absurd it bears repeating! Upon entering high school, Blake was placed in Math A (otherwise known as Math Sequential 1). Math A took all of 9th grade and ½ of 10th grade. Halfway through 10th grade, Blake took the Math A Regents. Then for the 2nd half of 10th grade and all through 11th grade, the next level was Math B (or Math Sequential 2). The Math B Regents would be taken at the end of 11th grade.

Blake was struggling with Math B. At the end of 10th grade, he had a D+. So going into 11th grade he was really at a disadvantage. Halfway through 11th grade, we made the determination it was not worth the stress to complete Math B. It was a very real possibility he was going to fail the regents. Blake did not need the Math B Regents to graduate. The decision was made to drop Math B and add Math AB or what was also known as Sequential Math 3. Blake finished out the year and ended up with a C.

He was looking forward to his senior year. He wanted to do all the fun things with his friends, but was really looking forward to just getting out of high school.

15

THE APPEAL

We knew we were in the right. We knew we were so wronged by the powers that be. I could not just turn my back and walk away. Now it was a choice between justice and paying another legal fee. I could not go down without a fight. I know it was such a cliché, but I felt like I was watching a movie with an incredibly stupid, illogical ending. I had all the proof anyone could ever need. We had expert testimony. We just had to win!

We **lost** on the appeal. The bottom line went pretty much like this. "The district must have done everything within its power because Blake passed all his classes."

Are you kidding me? Did I not show you proof he had failed. What about all the tutoring we paid for and the special programs we put him in. Nothing mattered. No one cared.

Appendix D is the part of the actual "Appeal Denied" letter.

16

BE AFRAID, BE VERY AFRAID! WHAT EVERY PARENT SHOULD KNOW ABOUT CHECKING GRADES, PROGRESS REPORTS, AND REPORT CARDS

I know I can't be the only one. But there are times when I've felt I had a target on my back that says, "Hit me!" By the time Blake was in Middle School, I was admittedly obsessed with his and his sisters' grades. Between all 3 of my kids, there have mistakes after mistake after mistake. If it weren't so sad, it would be comical.

During the Hearings, the district's attorney even accused me of "looking for problems." The following is just some of the mistakes we found:

1: Michelle's Spanish 3 final grade was incorrect. She was given a B and it should have been a B+. It took all summer and the beginning of the fall semester to rectify the problem.

2: Nicole was told she did not have to take the Math final if she had above an A average. The teacher told her she had to take the final because she did **not** have an A. Nicole and I re-checked the numbers for her. Re-checking a Math teacher's math! The Principal finally granted Nicole an exemption from the exam.

3: All of my kids had progress reports and report cards, at some point, with wrong grades and wrong comments. The excuse was that someone must have punched in the wrong number or remark. Over the years, it was punched in wrong at least 8 times.

4: Blake had an ASL class where, based on the teacher's contract, she erred in her math. It took 10 months to rectify that grade.

5: During the hearings, I was told Blake never failed a class. I have the original reports showing he had failed.

6: The district lied on Blake's IEP report card and said one of the objectives had been met, when in fact, it was never done at all. It was only after I questioned, that they quickly made it happen.

7: On one of his IEP reports, the school psychologist admitted to making a mistake while she was cutting and pasting. It took almost 4 months for the district to admit to that error.

8: Sometimes grades were not calculated properly, based on the contracts we had to sign.

9: There were constantly misspelled words on his IEP. A personal pet peeve of mine... (I hope you don't find any in this book!)

10: For one of the past projects Blake did, the percentages did not add up to 100%, another math error.

11: One year the final transcripts were printed wrong due to a computer error. The grades were right, but the class rankings were wrong!

Why did I make this a separate chapter? I needed to stress the importance that **mistakes happen**. Most are unintentional, but they affect your student's academics if gone unchecked. This is especially important if you have a student that has enough trouble keeping his head above water.

If you get contracts from the teachers, read and understand them.

The contracts should not just be a one-way street. Just as your child needs to be accountable, so should the teacher. We even got one excuse that this is the contact they have been using for years, so it is obviously appropriate. I pointed out flaw after flaw.

I am not saying you have to check every single grade, paper, or report, but once again; you have to trust your instincts, as well as listen to your child. If something doesn't look right or does not seem to make sense, sit down and re-do the math. If your child is insistent he thinks something is wrong, do not dismiss it. Follow through until you and your child are satisfied with the answers you are given. If you are still not sure, you must persist. Unfortunately, in my experience, most parents just give up. Every so often, it takes a lot of time and energy to get answers and sometimes life gets busy.

The district counts on the fact that the parent is just going to "go away".

17

THE COLLEGE SEARCH AND ACTS

Here is another situation where I found myself comparing my kids. I know it is wrong but they are so different.

For example, my oldest did just about everything that had to do with college, on her own. I don't think I even saw a college application except to help proofread her essay. My middle one was moderately involved, but needed much more help getting started. As for Blake, this was such an overwhelming task. Interestingly, the one area he needed less help than his sisters was his essay. He banged that out in no time. It came from his heart. The spelling, punctuation and grammar were another story, but that was to be expected.

Another example is what type of college we should look into, public or private. Even with two already in college, we did not qualify for any financial aid. Both my girls went to private schools, which was not the original plan. However, at that time, there was not one state school that had what they were looking for. We somehow made it work and the girls went to the schools that suited them best.

Blake was interested in TV Production and Broadcasting. He has taken these courses in high school and according to his instructors; he has a creative gift in this area. Blake is also very interested in playing basketball in college. The dilemma is this. There are state schools that have terrific TV programs but most are Division 3. Some of the private are Division 2. He does not think he could make Division 1. Blake's first choice of schools is wherever he can play ball. My husband and I are now in agreement that we don't want to pay the high price for private school since Blake is not the student his sisters are. All his applications were in on time. We were just waiting to get the results of his latest ACT grades.

Many professionals over the past few years had recommended Blake take the ACT exam instead of the SAT. There were many reasons, but the main one was the time factor. As part of Blake's IEP, he gets extra time (time and a half) when taking these type of exams. The ACT people approved this modification. The SAT would be a very long exam. Also the content of the ACT would be a better indicator of Blake's abilities.

Blake took the ACT three times. The first was in December of his junior year. He took it with a minimal amount of tutoring prep. His math tutor, Mr. C, was working with him for his regular math class so he just extended the subject matter. His scores did not surprise any of us. The discrepancy between the Math and English was classic Blake. Just as it was when he was tested back in 2nd grade.

His composite score was a 17 (Math – 24, Science - 19, English - 12, Reading - 14, Combined English/Writing - 11)

The second time was in April of his junior year. Again there was no real English tutoring though we did attempt it. One tutor was so wacky and over the top in the amount of homework she would give. The other tutor was very nice but had cats. Blake is allergic to them.

His composite score, the second time, was a 19 (Math – 24, Science - 20, English - 15, Reading – 15, Combined English/Writing - 15)

We tried to locate another English tutor. It was very difficult to find one that understood Blake's disability, one that could keep him motivated, one that was not boring.

Blake experienced two more tutors. One was very nice, but boring in her tone and manner and the other just did not get him. It was a sad state of affairs. His math tutor starting working with him again and also added the science section to his tutoring sessions.

The third time was the charm. Blake took the ACT for the final time in October of his senior year. This was it. We were sending these scores to the schools, good or bad. The exam was given over 2 days about 3 hours per day, one on one, with a reader.

His composite score, this last time, was a 23 (Math - 26, Science - 24, English - 20, Reading - 22, Combined English/Writing - 18)

In ten months, Blake was able to increase his composite score 6 points. I was so proud of him. Once again, thank goodness for Mr. C! I think I was more excited than Blake.

We received his scores in the mail approximately four weeks later. I quickly went on to some of the college websites to make sure they had received them. To my surprise some did not. We have since found out it could take up to four weeks for some schools to update their online information, after they have received the ACT/SAT grades.

We sent an email to one of the schools and they confirmed they had not yet received the scores. Now what do we do. They asked us if could fax them a copy of what we had received. The guidance counselor faxed it immediately.

I am very proud to say that the very next day the Assistant Director of Admissions sent Blake a wonderful email. Blake had been accepted to his first college!

The end result was that Blake applied to 13 schools and was accepted to 9 of them. He was even accepted to the Broadcasting Programs in 4 of the schools!

18

HERE WE GO AGAIN, IN REAL TIME!
(12TH GRADE)

The original title of this section was supposed to be "It Is Time". While writing this book, Blake was finishing the first quarter of his senior year. For the most part, things were going extremely well.

I know it is such a cliché, but where has the time gone? I felt like we have spent so much of Blake's high school years fighting. Twelfth grade was going to be so different. Blake was ready. No longer will we hear, "Blake needs to advocate for himself." I have been telling the powers that be for years (sorry to repeat myself) they will know when he is ready. To quote another cliché, " Be careful what you ask for."

For the first time ever, in Blake's educational career, ten weeks have gone by where I have not emailed or contacted a teacher for any reason. I did not even go to Meet the Teacher Night because we had to attend a business dinner. I felt a little guilty but Blake's a senior. I never missed Meet the Teacher with any of my kids. I purposely was hanging back from getting involved. Blake was more than ready and definitely willing to handle his own affairs.

However, if the truth be told, I knew in the back of my mind there is suppose to be this support system in place. After all, he has an IEP. If he were really in any kind of trouble academically, I would be notified. Even though this system, as detailed earlier, had failed miserably and often, I was certain this year would be different.

Here we go again....

Blake is taking a full load of classes and is even doubling up on

Economics and PIG (People In Government). Most students in our district only take one each semester. He is happy with his classes except English. He wanted to take Creative Writing, something he is very good at. However, it did not fit into his schedule. It did not fit because he elected to take College Astronomy. Class scheduling is constantly a problem in our school. The only class that fit was Intro to College Writing. In theory, this class should have been extremely helpful.

Problem one: The teacher who was supposed to teach the class was the same teacher Blake had for the first half of 9th grade. He failed with her and was dropped down to a self-contained English class. I convinced him that it was not the same type of class (there were no vocabulary tests) and she would probably be okay. We liked her.

Problem two: On the first day of class, the students were told Mrs. Sinto is still out on maternity leave and will not be back until after the New Year. Their interim teacher was Mrs. Goose. She had previously retired and was hired back for this temporary position.

Having two older children that had gone through the system, I knew at least one of them could help me understand why I was uncomfortable with Mrs. Goose, as Blake's teacher. Michelle (my oldest) immediately said that Mrs. Goose was tough and would have been a good teacher for her, but she did not think Mrs. Goose would "get" Blake.

Immediately, I put in a call to his Guidance Counselor (Mrs. House) and the Head of Special Ed (Mrs. Rice). Mrs. Rice told me she had actually been flooded with calls of concerned parents regarding this particular choice of replacement. I, like others, were told to give it a chance. Changes could always be made later.

Earlier, I spoke about the contracts teachers had the students and parents sign, so everyone would be on the same page, regarding class expectations. Blake and I signed his and he turned it in. This little fact will be important in just a bit.

The first assignment was to complete their personal essay for their college applications. I think everyone would agree this exercise could be extremely helpful. Mrs. Goose did the final edit. The students, then, needed to rewrite the essay and turn it in to be graded.

Blake was not really happy with the way Mrs. Goose edited his paper. She eliminated some points he felt were important. Though I agreed with him, I explained she was grading the paper, so he should make the changes she requested. I also assured him that we did not have to send the colleges this particular version.

Here is the poignant part to this episode. Blake received a 90 on his paper. I was thrilled. He was pissed (pissed is the most accurate way to describe his feelings at that moment). When I questioned him further, his answer was as follows, "Why didn't I get a 100? If she had more suggestions or ideas on how to improve my paper, why didn't she edit it some more? How am I suppose to get better if I don't know what changes to make?"

The quarter continues. Blake is excelling in Math, doing okay in Eco and PIG and holding his own in College Astronomy. We have been busy sending out college applications and trying to meet with basketball coaches. Blake made the Varsity basketball team! The Coach tells him, in the 13 years he has been coaching, Blake is the first person to make the team as a senior, after being cut as a junior. Things are going very well.

Halfway through the quarter, I receive Blake's progress report in the mail. Under English, it does not have the temporary teacher's name, only the original teacher. The comments are: More effort needed and homework often incomplete/not done. Blake came home from school and I went ballistic. I am furious with him. We are so far beyond getting homework done. He tells me he thinks he has turned everything in. Maybe he is missing one. He will check with Mrs. Goose tomorrow.

He does this and confirms he is only missing one assignment, which he hands in. **Missing one homework assignment is a far cry from "Often".**

One of the colleges, at the top of Blake's list, requires you to send your 1Q grades. We decide to possibly send all his schools the grades since he was doing well. Blake addressed the envelopes and handed them in to his Guidance Counselor (GC). He also asked her to let him know when she gets his grades. He wants to see them before they get sent out. She agreed.

Several weeks before the end of the quarter, Blake starts complaining about Mrs. Goose, the English teacher. They are definitely having some issues. Blake complains about the way he feels he is being treated. I don't hear anything from the teacher so it obviously is not a behavior problem. I am guessing they are just butting heads. I am determined to try and let them work it out, especially since I think he is doing well in the class. I have not heard otherwise, from anyone, and Blake seems to think his grades are okay.

About two weeks before the end of the quarter, I start to get this familiar uneasy feeling. I'm a bit nauseous; my heart races, my gut instinct tells me something is terribly wrong. I don't want to call the teacher so I email Mrs. Rice (Special Ed). After all, she is part of Blake's support team. I ask her if she can meet with Blake's teachers and see how he is doing. I told her that he and Mrs. Goose have been having issues and it is not good. She got back to me quickly and says she has not heard anything negative, so she guesses he is doing okay.

The following week, I am still troubled. I email his GC reminding her to please let us know Blake's grades before we send out his transcripts. I also give her a little background as to what has been going on in English class.

The last week of classes, Mrs. Goose tells Blake and others that they have an incomplete. Again he asks her why and is told he is missing another assignment.

At this point I need to clarify some things. Blake missed two days of classes taking his ACTs. Due to his modifications, he takes them in school over several days, three hours each day. He missed another day of school because we went on a college visit.

Of the assignments Blake was missing, one was *due* during the ACT and one was *given* during the ACT. Mrs. Goose told him he should have

given the assignment to another student to hand in and he should have **gotten** the other assignment from a homework buddy.

Though that sounds like a good policy to have in class, in reality, it depends on the quality of students, in that particular class. Blake has been with some of these kids for years. You would not want to trust them with your work or depend on them to give you accurate information. Many have issues more severe than his.

The quarter ends on a Friday 13th! Early the following week, **Blake is told by Mrs. Goose, that he has a "D" for the quarter; a "D" in Intro to College Writing, 1Q of senior year.** Blake was having what I would classify as a melt down. He was texting me, lashing out in words that are not fit for print. Angry would not even begin to describe how he was feeling toward Mrs. Goose. I told him to make sure he does not leave without getting a list of his grades.

I was totally blind-sided. How could this have happened? No communication from this teacher except the Progress Report that was a bit inaccurate. Where is Blake's IEP teacher? In fact, who is Blake's IEP teacher? Where was the follow up? Where was the support? The first time I don't follow up on some things, he once again falls through the cracks. Only now, this could affect his choice of colleges. It is not just about a simple grade; it is once again that the system has failed my son.

Interestingly, here are Blake's other grades:

Intro to College Math	A+
College Astronomy	C+
Eco	B
PIG	B
TV Production	A+

He is having one of his best quarters ever. Now what to do?

My first call was to Mrs. Rice. I left her a very detailed message. I still have not heard back from her after several days. My second call was to the GC to give her a heads up. I told Blake to find her and let her know what is going on. She could not meet with him at that moment so she had him make an appointment to see her the following day.

Blake came home from school exhausted, angry, depressed, defeated. It is such a sorry state of affairs, when one teacher's actions (or lack thereof) can have such a devastating effect.

This is a road we have traveled way too often. It is an agonizing step-by-step process to see where and how things started to unravel.

Step 1: Go through the grades for the quarter.

Step 2: Match up the grades with the actual work.

Step 3: Be sure you understand what the numbers mean and how they are used.

Step 4: Re-do the calculations.

Step 5: Review the contract.

When you start the process, you are not looking to place blame. You are looking for answers. As previously mentioned, honest mistakes have been made and are easily corrected. There have been times when I have questioned something and it was clear that Blake was at fault. There have also been several times where Blake was at fault, but the supposed "Support System" was broken. In those cases, Blake still suffered the consequences. There rarely was any accountability on the part of the teachers or administration.

I have been told that I am always looking for problems. There might be some truth to that, for very good reasons. If there had not been so many mistakes in the past, with all of my children, I would not feel obligated to follow-up or double check, especially when something doesn't ring true. Unfortunately, there are times when there is someone or something to blame.

Blake had about an 88 average for his tests/quizzes/writing/presentations. He then had a 47 for Homework and a 44 for Edit Notes. His average was a 60, an F! Mrs. Goose "generously" gave him a D, supposedly due to his effort. We realized in Step One that each of these sections was worth a third of the grade.

Realization #1: No wonder why Blake thought he was doing well. What he thought was the Main part of his grade was an 88. Nowhere in the contract does it spell out how students are being graded. It does not say Homework is worth one-third of the grade and Edit Notes are worth another one-third.

Realization #2: Blake had two zeros under Homework and two zeros under Edit Notes. He told me for the first time that Mrs. Goose does not accept any late work. You get a zero. Now I am starting to kick myself, for not getting involved immediately, after I received his progress report. I am also getting irritated again that I was not contacted by anyone.

Realization #3: The contract is very specific and contradicts her "No late work accepted" policy. According to the contract, the student has up to two weeks to hand in work that is incomplete. It does not specifically say, that even when you turn in the work, you will not get any credit for it!

Blake and I reviewed everything and talked about how he should approach the meeting with his Guidance Counselor. Though I knew this was an exercise he needed to go through, I also knew it was futile. The GC has no power to do anything and this particular GC usually sides with the teachers. Blake's GC has been great helping with college, but she has not been vocally supportive of Blake at all, during high school.

Just as an aside, I have my Master's degree in School Counseling and I decided not pursue this field. I realized the majority of the position, by design, is mostly scheduling classes and paperwork for college. Guidance Counselors, through no fault of their own, don't have time to hardly do anything else. Their caseloads are just too big. I always believe that decisions should be based on what is best for the child. In my opinion, with 45 years of experience in this district, this is more the exception than the rule.

Blake's GC meeting went as expected. She told him what he needed to do to help improve his grades. She told him not everything that went on in class needed to be written in the contract. She emailed me a similar story. I disagree 100% and told her so. Then what is the point of the contract?

My response to the GC was if the teacher changed her expectations from what was written on the contract, that I signed, she was responsible for notifying me of the change, preferably in writing. Why is that concept so difficult to understand or execute?

It is now a week since the quarter has ended. Technically, there is only one more week until the "grace period" is up. I asked Blake to be sure he finds Mr. Jack, the Asst. Principal, and schedule a meeting with him.

When Blake got home, he told me he was uncomfortable just walking into Mr. Jack's office and telling him the story from the beginning, so we went to plan B. I typed up a letter expressing all of our concerns. We included a copy of the Contract, the progress report, and two edit notes that the teacher would not accept.

There were several emails between Mrs. Short (Dept. Head), and me. All she wanted to do was have another meeting with Mrs. Goose. I just wanted some answers. I sent a very detailed note to Mr. Jack, basically re-hashing what I said earlier. One theme that is absent from Mrs. Short's emails is the word "contract". My entire argument is totally ignored. Mr. Jack at least took the time to listen to both sides.

The result of the bantering is that we will be having a meeting next week. It now seems clear to me, the Head of the Department can't look at one of her teacher's contracts, and determine whether or not, it is appropriate, without meeting with the parent. It seems clear to me, the Department Head can't meet with the Head of Spec. Ed and determine if Blake's IEP is being followed, without meeting with the parent. As stated in one of my responses, I feel, in this matter, I did not have to meet with anyone. It is your department. It is your teacher's wording in the contract. The wording is so specific; it could only be interpreted one way. Why do you need to waste my time and others for another meeting? As Department Head, are you incapable of making an executive decision and maybe, just once, do what is right by the student. Parents will think better of you if you are fair and not always one sided.

THE MEETING

I could have written the script for this meeting. Participating were the Assistant Principal, Guidance Counselor, Myself, the Head of the Dept, the Head of Spec Ed, and the teacher.

The teacher kept talking about all the wonderful things she has done to help the students. I said she is missing the point. The Department Head said it should be Blake taking responsibility. After all, he will have to be accountable in college. I said she is missing the point. The GC said no one is going to hold his hand when he goes away to school. I said she is missing the point. The Head of Spec Ed said nothing until after the Meeting. The Assistant Principal (AP) said we would need to look into this more. This, of course, is the "Reader's Digest" version of "The Meeting."

There were more emails back and forth and I told the AP I wanted to pursue this further. He was going to talk to the Principal and try and get, yet another meeting, together before the Christmas break. This did not end up happening.

In the meantime, Blake's first choice of schools wanted his 1Q grades. I did not want to send them with a D in English. This is why I was trying to push to get this issue resolved. The GC said she has never sent a note with a report card and didn't quite know what to say. She did not think it would look good for Blake to send a note that we were contesting a grade.

Out of frustration, I called the college and the admissions department was wonderful. I explained the story and the Rep did not seem to bat an eye. She told me to send a letter saying exactly what was going on, proof of his grades and any other supporting material. I did just that, including the original contract. Now we wait…

Two and a half weeks after school re-opened from winter break, I was finally able to schedule a meeting with the Principal, with the help of the AP. The three of us met for about an hour. During that meeting, I reiterated my concerns and was pleasantly surprised the Principal actually agreed with me on most of them.

Though he felt uncomfortable changing Blake's "D", he had another suggestion that amazed me. He offered to call the college directly and speak with the Admissions Counselor handling Blake's file. He said he would explain the situation, state how well Blake was doing 2Q and give his personal recommendation. According to him, he has done this twice in the past and it holds a lot of weight when the Principal calls on a student's behalf.

I agreed and was just hoping that it was not too little too late.

Two days later, I received an email from the Principal letting me know what he had said and to whom he spoke with.

Again we wait…

19

What Has Blake Taken Away From All Of This?

Blake's perspective

The comments I heard from Blake, most often, were these:

They are not listening to me.

They don't understand what I mean.

Why are they making me do this project?

That is not what they said.

I don't understand what they want from me.

They don't get it.

I can't help it.

I must be stupid if I can't get this right.

This is not helping me. No, I don't know what would help.

When I make some suggestions, they tell me to try it their way.

They keep saying the same things over and over again.

If I don't get it the first few times then just repeating yourself is not helpful.

Why is it that I know the answers in class, but fail the tests?

THERE WERE SOME POSITIVE MOMENTS:

Why didn't they explain it that way before? This makes sense now.

Calm explanation is much better than yelling.

If it is written down, I am more likely to finish it. However, sometimes I forget to write it down.

What makes sense to you may not make sense to me.

I don't have a problem.

What I ask you may not actually be what I want to ask you.

Sometimes I get my words mixed up or pronounce them wrong.

I never mind when someone corrects me. I do mind when they make fun or are condescending.

I am a good kid. I am very creative, athletic, fun, and caring.

I am a great brother, son and friend.

So I have trouble spelling, so what?

20

BLAKE'S OWN WORDS: HIS COLLEGE ACADEMIC ISSUES ESSAY

(BLAKE WROTE THIS AS HE REALLY WRITES AND SPELLS!)

The following is a slight exaggeration of an issue affecting my academic career. I was not properly diagnosed until 2½ years ago.

What is dyslexia? im going two try and explain it. Sum peeple say that when people are dyslexic they mess up letters and words and a bunch of other things including speling. This is sometimes true. I am Blake and I am dyslexic.

I have gone two a few doctors and I have ben classified as having dyslexia. I didn't no what it really ment butt I guess it just means that I have problems speling and that sometimes I mix up easy things weather is it the wrong word or the wrong leter. Four an example I sometimes mess up my "b" and "d", my "j" and "g", my "p" and "q", and my "4" and "9"or my "6" and "9". I don't know why that happens but sometimes if I am righting or typing ill spell out "beb" instead of "bed" or something like that.

I don't sea me being dyslexic as a problem but more of just something that makes me different from everybody else. I learn things differently and I am very creative. Spelchek is very helpful to.

Dys-lex-i-a: N – any of various reading disorders associated with the impairment of the ability to interpret spatial relationships or to integrate auditory and visual information. (I copied that exactly from the dictionary)

I was diagnosed in 2nd grade as Learning Disabled. In 9th grade, I was tested outside the school and diagnosed with Developmental Dyslexia reading at a 4th grade level. Since that time, I have been involved with the Wilson Reading program, many tutors and trying to "catch up". I am now in all regular classes including a college class. (Spell check and mom helped me with this section)

I am Blake and I am Dyslexic.

21

FROM A PARENT'S PERSPECTIVE

As a parent, this has been very frustrating. I feel most of what Blake has taken away from this has been negative. Though he has had a handful of absolutely wonderful teachers, the overwhelming majority did not understand him or the challenges he was facing. In their defense, a small minority wanted to help, but did not have the experience. However, the end result was the same, Blake continued to fall behind.

We all know that hindsight is 20/20, but in this case, I am hoping I might save many children, parents, and even teachers some heartache and give them the tools to move forward. Not all of my suggestions will be helpful to everyone and some may not even agree, but at least it is a starting point for the discussion.

My comments are in no particular order:

I feel there is too much wasted time in the classroom. This is not an attack on the teachers but rather on the administrators, school, and state officials. There has been so much pressure regarding the standardized testing, that the teachers are spending too much time teaching for the exam. Periodic testing may be okay, but the frequency of the testing is out of control!

Let's be honest about the standardized tests. Are they really "standardized"? Don't all states have different "standards"? New York State (NYS) Regents exams don't mean a thing, if you apply to a school outside of NYS. My children got into really good schools outside of New York. One of my daughters never took her Chemistry regents and all three of them never technically took a language regents, since NYS does not consider ASL a "real" language. (My oldest did take the Spanish regents, in addition to ASL)

The SATs and ACTs are a total waste of time and money. The amount of pressure on the student and on the parent is so unnecessary. Financially, the prep programs and individual tutors are expensive. They range in prices, from hundreds to thousands of dollars, depending on where you live and what program you choose. Individual tutors charge anywhere from $70 (which is rare) to $100+ an hour. I would estimate $90/hr is the norm where we live. I believe the original intent of these tests was to level the playing field and also to determine how successful a student will be, in their first year of college. I don't feel these tests accomplish their goals. I also strongly feel they should be eliminated.

I have seen a trend, over the past several years, in the many colleges we have visited, that some are moving away from placing such a high level of importance on these tests. However, they are still using them as a tool for granting scholarships, which I deem unfortunate.

I have often been told the reason for testing is to identify those students that need help. Could this be more insulting to the teachers? Even the not so good teachers can tell you which students need help. Blake was classified as Learning Disabled since he was in 2nd grade. Did we need to test him again and again? My oldest was an honor student. Did she constantly need to be tested? I don't believe so.

Blake's 4th grade English State Test (ELA) was graded as a Level 4 (749/800)! That meant, "Students consistently demonstrate understanding of written and oral text beyond the literal level. They can analyze and interpret a variety of texts, identify significant story elements, compare and synthesize information from related texts, and form insightful opinions, using extensive supportive details. Students' writing is well organized, thoroughly developed, and uses sophisticated and effective language, with few or no errors in spelling, grammar, or punctuation."

How did he accomplish such a feat? One of the teachers was helping him. He had a reader and a scribe. In 8th grade, he scored a Level 2 (630/800)! 650 was the minimum for meeting standards.

On Blake's 4th grade Social Studies Assessment he scored a 90/100, which also put him at Level 4. Again, he had a reader and a scribe. No one seemed to think this was a problem!

Many of the teachers, given to Blake, were tenured. Some were horrible. The whole tenure issue needs to be revamped. There were some great teachers that were not tenured. They stood up for the students or wanted to try something different. There were budget cuts and some great teachers were let go, even though they were better than some of those that were tenured. Teachers should not be fired because they were the last hired.

Tenure is defined as a noun meaning: 1 - appointment or period of appointment, and 2 - permanent status. The educational system obviously uses definition #2. Who else has permanent job security? For the most part, unless a teacher engages in the most flagrant of acts, they will always hold on to their position. Some are now saying that a teacher should be "graded" on their ability to increase a student's performance. I think this sounds great in theory, but it could be a very dangerous practice. "Grades" should be specific and measurable, not subjective. (Sounds like the IEP!) On the other hand, if you have a majority of the parents complain year after year about a particular teacher, it stands to reason there may be a significant problem that the district should address.

Our district, and I am sure it is the same in many others, say they want parents, teachers, and students to work as a team. I believe they mean, "as long as the parent does not rock the boat". The parent, who questions, is seen as "a problem" that must be dealt with. I feel this is the main reason most parents don't speak up. They are afraid the teacher will somehow "take it out" on their child.

I have had many teachers and administrators say to me, "Blake needs to advocate for himself." In my observation, when Blake did so, he was not taken seriously. The automatic assumption was that Blake was not doing enough and needed to do more.

We pay our taxes. Our taxes pay the public school salaries. I think there are many teachers and administrators that should show the parents more respect. I know teaching is a tough profession, but if you are not cut out for it, you should not be teaching. When a teacher is not doing well, they are given "professional support", maybe even some mentoring. I guess I am tired of my child being the guinea pig while a teacher is being trained.

My son has had his share of unnecessary homework assignments, ridiculous projects, and wasted time in class watching movies. They were reading a book in English class and spent 4 days watching the film. They were given projects where the teacher wanted several of them to get together after school. Now I understand what the teacher was trying to do, but did she really think out all the details? Here we had a group of kids, with all different afternoon schedules. No one drove, so now the parents needed to get involved. We had to now figure out the parent schedules as well. Of course, some kids did more work than others, but they all got the same grade. How is this fair? The excuse I was given was, "The students need to work in groups so when they go to college or out into the business world they will be better prepared."

I don't think I need to tell you my response, but here it is. When they go to college, for the most part, they will be living on campus or near each other and can get around by themselves. In the business world, more than likely, they would work in groups, at work. If you want them to work in groups, then let them have quality time in class.

Here is a question I did ask constantly. "What is the point of this assignment/project? What do you expect them to get out of it?" There were so many times when the answer was "this is what they have been doing for the past few years and we feel it is a good assignment for them". I was hardly ever given a satisfactory answer. Occasionally, I was surprised that there was a method to the madness and I was appreciative of the teacher who took the time to explain.

A big complaint among many teachers is the low salary. I believe that varies greatly between districts, but I don't feel teachers should get raises automatically because they have tenure. Sorry I mentioned the "T" word again. On the flip side, I don't feel teachers' salaries should be frozen just because they have made it to a certain level of pay.

I feel college graduates, after only one or two semesters of student teaching, are really not ready to take on the demands of the classroom. I would like to see an intermediate step, with possibly a mentor. How long this step takes would depend on the "nubie", maybe a semester or maybe even a full year. This would give them day-to-day support, but not leave the students at their mercy. It would also give parents a higher comfort level when they hear their child has the "new" teacher.

We live in a decent size district You would think there would be a certain level of consistency between schools. Sadly, this is not the case. Classes are different. Requirements are different. Sports are handled differently. I can understand differences among districts, but within the same district? This makes no sense and only adds to the confusion and frustration among the parents and students.

Where do you go if you have a problem? First, you contact the teacher. If you are not satisfied, you might go to their supervisor. If still not satisfied, you can go to an administrator. After that, someone at the district level. And after that…the lines get a bit fuzzy.

How long should you have to wait to get an issue resolved? As I mentioned in an earlier chapter, some of our issues were never resolved. They just kept getting moved around from person to person. Remember one issue took 10 months!

For those of you whose children have an IEP (Individual Education Plan), this has been a major Achilles heel for us. An IEP is a formal, legal document. In my opinion, there is no "I" in IEP. The IEP comments are written from a drop down menu. The goals are supposed to be specific and measurable. A GOAL *(N)* is defined as: 1-target area, 2-aim, 3-score, 4-successful shot, 5-race's end. An OBJECTIVE *(N)* is defined as: a goal. OBJECTIVE *(Adj)* is defined as: 1-free of bias, 2-based on facts, 3-observable, and 4-existing independently of mind.

One example: The main objective in high school for Blake was to do his homework. The Goal, as explained in previous testimony, was for Blake to bring home his homework 75% of the time. Though on the surface this seems okay, but with closer examination, it makes no sense. First, does it matter if Blake brought his homework home? Shouldn't it be more important he hand the homework in? Second, why is the goal only 75%? Does that mean he doesn't need to bother the other 25% of the time. Wouldn't it make more sense if the goal read "Blake should hand his homework in 95% of the time?" This would now be specific and measurable. **You should be aware that, on the IEP, 75-80% as a goal is considered MASTERY.**

Another example: A goal is something that should take time to work towards. Two of Blake's goals were for him to read a list of 10 words. He was given the words; he read them, goal accomplished. A one shot deal! As seen in the earlier testimony, we later found out that the words were actually from 1st through 3rd grade. Blake was in 10th! When he was able to read the list, wouldn't one think that a more advanced list would be added and his goal updated?

Here is my bottom line to parents. Unfortunately, we are in a system where just questioning something becomes adversarial. You have to know your child. If you have been cooperating with the district and you still are not satisfied, for the sake of your child, you have to **push the issue.** You might get lucky and get the help you need. You might not. You have to **trust your instincts**.

You are your child's best advocate, even when they are in high school (and even possibly in college). Yes, they have to take on some responsibility. Not all children can do that just because they are now in 9th grade. Some won't be ready until they go to college. **That's okay!** You know your child. As a parent, **you have a right to step in and expect answers to your questions.** As a parent, you need to **respect the teacher**, as they should toward you. The same is true for the student.

Write everything down. Every conversation, phone call, email, letter, everything. **Keep yourself organized** either by dates and/or topic. **Save everything!** Report cards, progress reports, IEP reports, and notes.

Here is one example of why this is so important. During one of the hearings, the district's lawyers made a comment that was not true. They claimed, based on Blake's transcript (which only displays the final grades), that he never failed any classes. Blake had previously been in several classes where he was not performing well. I have the report cards with the failed grades. If I did not have that paper work, I would not have been able to prove otherwise.

Unfortunately in our case, the hearing officer and the appellate hearing officer chose not to pay any attention to this detail.

However, things don't always turn out as planned. It is, at these times, when you need to **be persistent**; you need to **be relentless**. You may feel angry... angry with yourself, your spouse, your child, the teacher, everyone involved. You may be overwhelmed that your child is still having issues and there has not been any resolution or accountability. You may feel hopeless, helpless and depressed. You may feel alone. You may feel like no one is listening. You may feel like your friends are getting tired of hearing you complain. And you may be right! But for your own sanity and for your child's sake, **KEEP TALKING!** Talk to anyone and everyone who will listen. Your strength is going to come from the fact that you are doing what is in the best interest of your child. NO ONE can ever fault you for that!

22

In Conclusion

When Blake was tested for the first time in **2nd grade**, it was clear that "lags were found in reading, especially in basic skills which were not consistent with potential. Blake is losing ground. He is not hold is own." **(Yes there was a typo in the report!)**

The District's recommendations were:

1: Blake should be classified for special education services and receive a self contained (**another typo**) language arts block in the resource room.

2: Behavior modification techniques should be used to modify hyperactivity and improve focus on tasks.

3: Parents should review test findings with their pediatrician to determine if additional medical interventions would be helpful to manage ADHD related behaviors.

My reaction:

Recommendations need to be more specific, more INDIVIDUAL. Hyperactivity was never a real issue. I did not think Blake needed meds or that he was ADHD. I felt there was something else going on.

Several months later we did take Blake to a Neurologist. He suggested that Blake might have ADD but not ADHD. It was mild enough so no medication was needed at that time. He also stated, "Blake's reading impairment is consistent with a primary reading disorder."

When Blake was in **5th grade**, I brought him to another neurologist, for a second opinion. He, too, concluded possible mild ADD, no medication needed, but also went on to state, "There may be an underlying language-based learning disability or reading disability as well." The doctor was very clear that Blake was not ADHD, although he was an extremely active 10-year-old boy, which is very different.

He told me Blake had all these wonderful attributes. He told me not to worry. Blake would be successful. He will have friends and maybe a family. Unfortunately, Blake's strengths are not typically what school emphasizes. The doctor explained that my job, as a parent, is to be sure Blake got whatever services he needed so he doesn't fall too far behind. Even more importantly, we need to keep Blake's self-esteem in tact. This man's words resonated in my head every single day. It is what kept me sane on the worst of days.

For years, we listened to the Professionals and did what they told us to do. I was frustrated because I felt like no one was listening to me. They were not seeing what I was seeing at home. Call it women's intuition or mom's instinct, but I knew I was right.

As pushy and demanding as some in the district felt I was, one of my regrets is that I did not push harder earlier. There is definitely some guilt that maybe I could have helped Blake sooner, so he would not have had such a hard time.

The biggest mistake I made, according to my attorney, is that I did not sue earlier. When you sue the district, you can only go back **two** years. Nothing before that mattered even though I had all this information both positive and negative.

Believe it or not, there is a silver lining in all of this.

Blake is a happy, well-adjusted college student. He has lots of frien is still involved with sports and is very creative. He looks at thing sees things differently than most. He writes with his heart on his What you see is what you get. Blake will always struggle "English", but is confident enough to ask what something say spell a word he does not know. He has had his share of life disappointments and deals well with adversity. I feel his Dyslexia has made him a stronger and more patient individual. Sometimes dealing with frustration is an issue, but thankfully Blake has a great sense of humor and a great sense of self.

As his Mom, I am so proud of the person Blake is and how far he has come. I am excited to see where life will take him.

23

I Had To Add This: Good Things Come To Those Who Wait!

Blake started college in upstate New York and was accepted into a Communications Program majoring in Broadcasting. He desperately wanted to try and succeed on his own, without any assistance.

Classes seemed to be going well. He was working part time for the sports program and there were many friends.

Then, one day, I got a text message from him near the end of his first semester. He was very excited. It beautifully summed up the last 10+ years. I will apologize in advance for the language, but I think it is important to understand Blake's level of frustration with his academics.

*"I got a F******g A in College English! F*** my HS teachers!"*

Now of course, he did not mean all his HS teachers, but his comment was filled with raw, real, true emotion. I asked him if I can use the quote in the book and he said "yes!".

This college English professor saw potential in Blake. He will always have issues with spelling, grammar and punctuation, but all of that can be fixed. What is more important than the mechanics, is the actual getting your thoughts down on paper.

Blake's essays this semester have been funny, thought provoking and emotional. He has that rare quality to draw you in, surprise and entertain you. I thank this professor for building on Blake's self-esteem where the written word is concerned. He is taking English 102 with this same professor.

Overall, Blake finished his 1st semester with a 3.25 GPA, without any modifications. Second semester looks to be a bit more difficult but we are all optimistic.

Special Thank-you's!

I want to thank my family [my husband Charles, my daughters Michelle and Nicole, my parents A&B, my sister LML, some cousins (LS and SA) and aunts] for putting up with the long hours I have spent over the past 12 years, not only working on this book (for the past 3½ years) but in trying to do what is right, regarding Blake and school.

I need to thank my dearest friends, which have put up with my ramblings, when things have gone wrong, which they often did. (BF, DS, MZ, CT, EB, BK, BR, SP, APL)

There are some teachers/administrators that have gone above and beyond. They realized there was something special about Blake and tried to figure out the best way to help him succeed. I can't thank these people enough:

Elementary: K-MM, 2nd-DB, 3rd-KM, 4th-DR, 5th-TC & EF (The first time Blake actually tried to read a book and enjoyed it, was in your English class!).

Middle School: Science-SW, Eng-NB, Principal-DB

I need to make special mention of Blake's Math teacher "BC" (and 4 yrs of tutoring!) I don't know where Blake would be without you! Your patience, sense of humor, and calm manner was exactly what he needed.

High School: Eng-GA, US-EP, Govt-EK, TV-HF, Sp Ed-KR, Guidance-MH, Asst. Principal-TJ (You are one of the best things that ever happened to the high school. Please keep looking out for the students. They need more advocates like you!)

I want to thank AC and JS, our attorneys, and their staff for helping us to sue the school district. We did not win (nor did we win on the appeal) but I finally got the appropriate help for Blake.

I also want to thank CM, our student advocate, who was able to come to a meeting and help guide us. She also was a witness to several of the atrocities we had to deal with.

Another important thank you goes to Dr. M for testing Blake, listening to our plight and properly diagnosing his "disability".

This project could not have been done without the great staff at Apple. A special Thank You to Hank, Jean Marie, Maersk, Marco, Tom, Jon and the rest of the trainers.

The IDA-NY (International Dyslexia Association of NY, Now called Everyone Reading NY) and the IDA national chapter was more help than anyone could ever imagine. Diana, you were always a wealth of information and guidance. The conference was a blessing. I was able to learn so much, in a short amount of time, because of this organization.

Lastly, this project would have never been completed without the help of my proofreaders and editors (IK, LC, LS, PL, JL, BF).

A Final Word

I had to include this email that my son recently sent us from college. It's Blake's email to us and my husband's response.

Email From Blake EXACTLY As He Wrote It To Us:

Broadcasting- I just got my second exam back in broadcasting and i got an 84% on it!! :) I also got my reaction paper back for broadcasting today and i got a 20-20 on it!! that grade is 20% of my final grade :) ll

Math- Although I started off slow i got a 95% on my last quiz and i believe im going to get a good grade on the exam that i took on wednesday.

:) think i found my stride in college

miss you guys

Charles' Response:

Happy at college…wonderful

Getting good grades…gets a car

"miss you guys"…produces a tear

Being able to spell "Stride"…Priceless

APPENDIX A

Post Hearing Memorandum
(11/7/08)

IN THE MATTER OF AN IMPARTIAL HEARING, UNDER THE IDEA BROUGHT BY Charles AND Elaine Mellon

ON BEHALF OF Blake, Petitioners

-against-

SCHOOL DISTRICT , Respondent

POST-HEARING MEMORANDUM OF LAW OF SCHOOL DISTRICT IN SUPPORT OF A DENIAL OF ALL OF THE PARENTS' CLAIMS

I.   PRELIMINARY STATEMENT

("the District") hereby submits this Post-Hearing Memorandum of Law in Support of a Denial of All of the Claims of Claimants ("Mrs. M") and C.M.("the Parents") in the above-captioned Demand For Due Process Hearing ("the Complaint") concerning their son Blake, who is currently an eleventh grade student in-District. All of the Parents' claims concern only one School Year, which is School Year 2007-2008.

II.   STATEMENT OF FACTS AND ISSUE PRESENTED

The facts and issues presented in the Complaint and elucidated at the hearing sessions held on this Complaint will not be set forth at length in this section of the Memorandum of Law, but rather will be detailed in the Statement Of Applicable Law and Facts Proven At Hearing Section, <u>infra.</u> A hearing began on this matter on May 1, 2008, and was continued on May 5, 14, 20, June 12, 23, August 12, 27, and October 6, 2008. Suffice it to say that the Parents have not proven at hearing any of the claims set forth in their Complaint and are entitled to no relief.

The Complaint sets forth the following demands for relief concerning School Year 2007-2008, none of which demands were substantiated at the hearing:

- Annulment of the current IEP

- Provision of an appropriate IEP, developed with the equal participation of the Parents and consideration of Dr. X's neuropsychological evaluation and the AT evaluation. The IEP shall address Blake's academic, social, emotional and physical management needs. Current, accurate PLEPs (including the diagnosis of dyslexia and other diagnoses as indicated in the herein referenced evaluation) shall be included. Necessary methodologies, appropriate, measurable goals to address the needs indicated, and an appropriate transition plan shall be developed and reflected on the IEP.

- Provision of an assistive technology evaluation, and implementation of recommendations as well as goals to address those recommendations.

- Provisions of the Wilson Reading Program, by an experienced individual certified and qualified Level II or trainer, of the Parent's choosing, for a minimum of one hour daily at the convenience of the family.

- Provision of extended school day academic intervention services to remediate all content areas. [The District shall pay for the continuation of the current tutor's services.]

- Provision of an intensive extended school year reading program of the Parent's choosing.

- Reimbursement for the reading instruction that the Parents paid for privately.

- Reimbursement for the academic tutoring that the Parents paid for privately.

- Reimbursement for the independent neuropsychological evaluation that the Parents paid for privately.

- Payment of the Parents' attorneys fees and expenses associated with representation in this matter.

- Development of an appropriate plan of transition that includes goals and objectives and services designed to assist the student in achieving those goals and objectives.

- Provision of any further relief that the Hearing Officer deems just and proper.

It is important to note that there has been no allegation by the Parents that any of the teams in the Committee on Special Education ("CSE") Meetings, out of which the IEPs in issue emanated, were not properly constituted or that the Parents' participation in the CSE process was in any way denied.

In addition, by stipulation of counsel on the last hearing date, the second to last Complaint Paragraph concerning transition planning has been waived by the Parents. See Tr. at 1547-1548. Moreover, Item 3 of the Complaint relating to Assistive Technology Evaluation has been largely, if not completely, mooted by the provision of such Evaluation. See District Exhibit 20 in evidence. And, the Parents did not demonstrate any deficiency in the implementation of that Evaluation. Similarly, the request for the Wilson Reading Program has also been mooted in that the District has informed counsel that Blake's current schedule contains the availability of Wilson Reading Program on a 1:1 basis in three out of six cycle days of Resource Room.

In any event, the following Statement of Applicable Law and Facts Proven At Hearing illustrates that none of the relief sought by the Parents should be awarded as a matter of law and fairness.

III. STATEMENT OF APPLICABLE LAW AND FACTS PROVEN AT HEARING

The legal standard governing the Parents' requests for reimbursement of the costs of tutoring, remedial reading services, and of a private evaluation is set forth in <u>School Committee of Burlington v. Dep't of Education</u>, 471 U.S. 359 (1985) and <u>Florence County School District Four v. Carter</u>, 510 U.S. 7 (1993). Under the three-part test established by the United States Supreme Court in <u>Burlington/Carter</u>: "A board of education may be required to reimburse parents for their expenditures for private educational services obtained for a student by his or her parents if (1) the services offered by the board of education were inadequate or inappropriate, <u>and</u> (2) the services selected by the parent were appropriate, <u>and</u> (3) equitable considerations support the parents' claim" <u>Id.</u>. (emphasis added). As the Parents fail on each prong of the above test, they may be awarded no relief.

Under New York Education Law § 4404 (1)(c), the school district has the burden of proving the adequacy and appropriateness of the educational programs it has provided, while the parents seeking reimbursement for unilateral placement or private services rendered on behalf of their child bear the burden of persuasion as to the parents' selected educational program's adequacy and appropriateness.[1]

Here, the record shows that the District has more than fulfilled its burden to demonstrate that a free and appropriate public education ("FAPE") was provided by the IEPs in issue as created by the CSE. In addition, the Parents failed to demonstrate the appropriateness of the

---

1   In <u>Schaffer v. Weast</u>, 546 U.S. 49 (2005), the United States Supreme Court determined that in the absence "of a special state law or regulation setting forth a special IEP-related burden of persuasion," the burden of persuasion to challenge an IEP was placed on the party seeking relief, which generally places the burden of persuasion on the parents. <u>Id.</u> at 70. New York State, however, amended its Education Law in 2007 by "placing the burden of proof upon the school district during an impartial hearing, except that a parent seeking tuition reimbursement for a unilateral placement would continue to have the burden of proof regarding the appropriateness of such placement." <u>See</u>, <u>Board of Education of Minisink Valley Central School District</u>, No. 08-051 at fn. 18 (citing Educ. Law § 4404(1)(c), as amended by Ch. 583 of the Laws of 2007).

private services for which they seek reimbursement and it was shown at hearing that equitable considerations further call for the full rejection of the Parents' claims.

As fully detailed and demonstrated below, the record clearly indicates that the District has bent over backwards to provide this child, who has never failed a course and has advanced year to year, with more than a FAPE in the four separate IEPs created to meet his needs for School Year 2007-2008. FAPE has also been demonstrated by the progress reasonably expected to be made by the program in these IEPs, which progress has been made by this child. The District's many educators' course of dealing with Blake and Mrs. M also demonstrates reasonableness and concern, which contributes to a FAPE having been provided.

Indeed, if there has been any problem with the IEPs or their implementation, which we strongly contend there has not been, it has been occasioned by the incessant attempted interventions of Mrs. M and by the Parents' refusal time and time again to allow the Wilson Reading Program to be inserted into this child's schedule. Furthermore, a general lack of cooperation with the District by the Parents has been strongly shown.

A. <u>A FAPE HAS BEEN PROVIDED BY THE CSE IN THE FOUR IEPs PROMULGATED FOR SCHOOL YEAR 2007-2008, WHICH IEPs WERE TAILORED TO MEET THE CHILD'S INDIVIDUAL NEEDS AND RESULTED IN THE CHILD'S SATISFACTORY PROGESS</u>

A FAPE has been provided by the CSE in the four IEPs promulgated for School Year 2007-2008, which IEPs were tailored to meet the child's individual needs and resulted in satisfactory progress by the child.

As set forth by the Second Circuit, the central purpose of the Individuals with Disabilities Education Act ("the IDEA") is to "ensure that all children with disabilities have available to them a free and appropriate public education that emphasizes special education and related services designed to meet their unique needs." See Frank G. v. Board of Education of Hyde Park, 459 F.3d 356, 372 (2d. Cir. 2006) (citing 20 U.S.C. § 1400(d)(1)(A-B)).

In Board of Education Of Hendrick Hudson Central School District v. Rowley, 458 U.S. 176 (1982), the U.S. Supreme Court set forth a twofold inquiry to ascertain if a FAPE has been provided. That inquiry is: "(1) whether the state complied with the procedural requirements of the IDEA; and (2) whether the challenged IEP was substantively appropriate or 'reasonably calculated to enable the child to receive educational benefits.'" Id. at 206-207, quoted in M.C. ex rel. B.C. v. Rye Neck Union Free School Dist., 2008 WL 4449338, *11 (S.D.N.Y. 2008)[2].

Under 20 U.S.C. § 1414(d)(1)(A)(ii), an adequate IEP must include:

> a statement of measurable annual goals, including benchmarks or short-term objectives, related to...meeting the child's...needs that result from the child's disability to enable the child to be involved in and progress in the general curriculum and meeting each of the child's other educational needs that result from the disability... cited in Rye Neck, supra. at *11

Even where there has been a procedural defect in its promulgation, which is not in issue here, the IEP is not legally inadequate unless the defect (a) impedes the child's right to FAPE; (b) significantly impedes the parents' opportunity to participate in the decision making process regarding the provision of a FAPE to the child; or (c) causes a deprivation of educational benefits to the child. See Grim v. Rhinebeck Cent.

---

2 The decision in Rye Neck by District Judge Seibel is an Order Adopting Report and Recommendation of United States Magistrate Judge Lisa Margaret Smith in its entirety which was prepared for the consideration of United States District Judge Brieant. As stated in the Order, "a district court reviewing a Magistrate Judge's report and recommendation 'may accept, reject, or modify, in whole or in part, the findings or recommendations made by the magistrate judge.' Id. (citing 28 U.S.C. § 636(b)(1)(c)).

<u>School Dist.</u>, 346 F.3d 377 (2d Cir. 2003) (citing 20 USC § 1415(f)(3)(E)(ii)).

There is no defect, procedural or otherwise, in the IEPs at issue. The District has in no way failed to deliver a FAPE to this child, and has not impeded the child's right to one. Likewise, the District did in no conceivable way impede the Parents' opportunity to participate. Indeed, the interaction between Mrs. M and the District was quite to the contrary. The District gave the mother much more than ample opportunity to participate in the education of Blake. In fact, the record shows that Mrs. M attempted to lead the District in the management of Blake's studies and curriculum, and asked for tests to be re-administered and contested Blake's grades routinely.

Proof of that "lead" role attempted to be taken by Mrs. M in directing her son's education is found throughout the hearing. <u>See</u>, <u>e.g.</u>, District's Exhibit 22 in evidence, Jeffery Email J-95, in which email Mrs. M states concerning the first 2007-2008 IEP Meeting: "Unlike the first meeting where Mrs. Rice was chairing, I will have my own agenda that I would like addressed." <u>See</u> <u>also</u> Tr. at 412-419, which contains testimony by Mr. Jack, the Assistant Principal at Blake's school, of: (1) a placement change occasioned by Mrs. M; (2) the student's upset at learning that he received a grade of 83 on a project, a grade which Mr. Jack characterizes as "mastery," (3) the rejection by Mrs. M of the Wilson Reading Program on four occasions; (4) Mrs. M having been encouraged to have Blake attend extra help sessions "at a low ball estimate of 25 times," between Mr. Jack and Blake's other teachers; (5) all of the IEP meetings with Mrs. M having been "very lengthy and that two hours was certainly short for some of the CSE meetings that we had" while "most [other CSE meetings] last 45 to 55 minutes."[3]

---

3   Other evidence of Mrs. M's attempted control over her son's educational process is found in Email J 180 in evidence where Mrs. M states: "I have another request that Mrs. Obie not be part of the CSE team"; in Email J 261, where on the last line of that page, Mrs. M asks for "a 1:1 [proctor] with someone [B] is comfortable working with"; and Emails J 257, J 205, J 202, J 185, J 170, J 106, and J 100, where Mrs. M actively is advocating for retaking or re-grading of B's tests.

In addition, further evidence of more then full participation by the Parents is found in Mrs. M's rejection out of hand of what appears to be the reasonable suggestion by Mr. Jack of "Circle Sheets" to increase Blake's organizational abilities. Tr. at 217-219, discussing the Manna Email M-46, which emails are part of District's Ex.-16 in evidence. Moreover, the hearing officer should also consider the plethora of emails between Mrs. M and the educators. The District will not recount the sum and substance of each and every email sent by Mrs. M and the responses thereto by the District representatives, namely, among others, Mrs. Rice, Ms. Manna, Ms. Gilley, Ms. House, the Guidance Counselor, and Mr. Jack. Nevertheless, it is important to note that, without objection from the Parents, the District admitted into evidence a plethora of emails totaling 697 pages. This total is in addition to the large number of phone calls made of these educators, especially Mr. Jack. This total number of emails does not include any emails after the hearing began on May 1, 2008, of which there are many, and is comprised of Ex. D-14, the emails with Ms. Rice, marked R1-R61, Ex. D-15, the emails with Ms. Gilley marked G1-G191, Ex. D-16, the emails with Ms. Manna marked M1-M102, Ex. D-17, the emails with Ms. House marked H1-H10, and Ex. D-22, the hundreds of emails with Mr. Jack marked J1-J333.

There can be no dispute that almost 700 pages of emails with Mrs. M before May 1, 2008, as admitted into evidence, represents and extraordinarily voluminous amount. <u>Accord</u>, Tr. at 291 where Ms. Gilley testified that the 191 pages of emails she had with Mrs. M is "at least seven to ten times more than most parents," The proliferation of emails also indicates several things: (1) Mrs. M much more than fully participated in the formulation of the IEPs in issue at this hearing and in between IEP meetings to make sure all aspects of the child's program were suited to the child's individual needs and properly implemented; and (2) Mrs. M attempted to and did at times micro-manage and/ or lead the development and implementation of this child's program, including but not limited to numerous requests for test re-taking or grade reevaluating, numerous requests for teacher changes, or changes in specific classes, and many rejections of the numerous instances where the District attempted by every means to fit the Wilson methodology into Blake's schedule.

Therefore, the District's course of dealing with the Parents in continually granting them every conceivably helpful modification, e.g., offering Wilson, changing Blake's classes and teachers often, and in even adding testing accommodations not required by the IEP (See discussion infra, at fn. 5), also demonstrates the District's clear-cut provision of FAPE to this child.[4] Thus, in no way did the District deprive the child of any educational benefits. Rather, it was the mother herself who rejected the numerous recommendations by the District to have the Wilson methodology inserted into the child's program. See Tr. at 412-419. Accord, Tr. at 423-424 where Mr. Jack testified that the District had no issue with the X Report and specifically, as to the Wilson Program recommended by X, "we have no problem offering that. We wanted to offer that. It was not an issue for any of us." Id. Accordingly, the District cannot be forced to pay for Wilson remedial home tutoring because it provided a FAPE to this child, offered Wilson for this child, and in fact, it was Mrs. M herself who blocked the provision of those services during the school day to Blake.

1: <u>THESE IEPS WERE FASHIONED TO CREATE A REASONABLE AND APPROPRIATE PROGRAM TAILORED TO MEET THE CHILD'S NEEDS WITH MORE THEN COMPLETE PARTICIPATION BY THE PARENTS</u>

In what amounts to a comprehensive and successful effort to tailor a program to meet the individual needs of this student, there were

---

4   In addition to the District's clear provision of a FAPE for this child, the equities clearly do not favor the Parents in their less then cooperative bombarding approach to dealing with the District. Similarly, this course of dealing helps the District to demonstrate that the equities favor it in its supremely reasonable and patient approach to every complaint about Blake's program brought to its attention by Mrs. M, often on more than a daily basis. See discussion infra at Part C hereof.

four separate CSE Committee (or Subcommittee) Meetings concerning this child's program in School Year 2007-2008, at which IEPs were promulgated with more than complete participation by the Parents. An examination of the four separate IEPs constructed for Blake concerning this one School Year demonstrates that the District has more than met the statutory requirements and that the child's education indeed was tailored to meet his individual needs[5]. Blake's IEPs created by the CSE can be described as follows:

In the IEP dated February 12, 2007, which is District Exhibit 2, the CSE sets forth that the child is classified as learning disabled and is to receive Resource Room, a Special English Class, and a Special Social Studies Class. In addition, Blake also was to receive testing accommodations to meet his needs consisting of extended time, directions read and explained, recordings of answers in test booklets, and the use of a word processor. In the Comments Section of this IEP starting on page 4, it is clearly indicated that all of the required participants were present at this CSE Meeting and that the Meeting was convened because "[t]he student's mother requested an increase in

---

5   The record of the hearing also demonstrates that these reasonable IEPs were properly and consistently implemented by the District and meet all FAPE requirements. As noted above, the many class and teacher changes initiated by Mrs. M, the almost 700 pages of emails between Mrs. M and the educators, and the testimony of Ms. Gilley and Ms. Manna demonstrate the reasonableness, care and concern with which the IEPs were implemented. For example, Ms. Gilley, Blake's Resource Room teacher testified that she generally emailed Mrs. M weekly with progress reports from all of Blakes teachers, Tr. at 322, 331-332, and Ms. Manna, Blake's Special Education Social Studies teacher, testified that she had not previously "had a parent communicate with email with the frequency that Mrs. M does." Tr. at 197.

Furthermore, the hearing demonstrates the consistent involvement of Mrs. M in the implementation of the IEPs. See Tr. at 322, 291 (Ms. Gilley testified that she had seven to ten times the usual number of emails with Mrs. M), and 197.

Also, the testimony of Ms. Abeles, Blake's English teacher, demonstrates that testing accommodations additional to those required in the IEPs were implemented at Mrs. M's request, including preparing for Blake and providing him with vocabulary words in context on all of his tests. Tr. at 925-927.

special education services as she believes he requires a more restrictive and supportive program in order to meet his academic potential." Id.

The Comments further indicate a thoughtful and thorough sharing of ideas at the CSE Meeting on the kind of Social Studies Class which would meet this child's needs. They also indicate that Mrs. Rice, the Special Education Director at the high school where Blake attends, "suggested that the student might benefit from the Wilson Reading Program but wondered if scheduling would allow for his participation in the program this year." It is then reported that "[h]is mother did not think this would be practical at this time." Id.

Other issues also discussed reasonably and comprehensively by both the Parents and the Team at the February 12, 2007 CSE Meeting included the roles of Study Lab and Resource Room in Blake's program, the student's goals and objectives, and test modifications, concerning which "his mother provided input." Id. In addition, it is also noted in this Comments Section that the "student should be encouraged to regularly attend extra help sessions provided by his teachers." Id.

The testimony of Rice further supports that this first IEP in issue is tailored to meet Blake's individual needs, including the discussions by the CSE Team which went into the decision to put Blake into self contained English and Social Studies Classes. See Tr. at 33-35. Moreover, Ms. Rice confirms that she had indeed prior to the February 14, 2007 CSE Meeting recommended the Wilson Reading Program for Blake despite not having had a documented decoding problem because "mom reported it," and "mom reported that it had been a concern in previous years. We offered it at that time without documentation at the end of an IST meeting." See Tr. at 38. And, Ms. Rice continues, at the end of a prior Instructional Support Team ("IST") Meeting (held in November 2006), "we did offer to provide more testing because we didn't…have documentation. And we also offered the Wilson program." Id. at 39.

Ms. Rice further confirms that Mrs. M turned down the Wilson methodology at the February 2007 IEP meeting and testifies: "[A] lthough it was offered it was discussed that he could choose to take it at some later date." Tr. at 40. A more than full opportunity for Mrs. M to participate at this Meeting, which lasted approximately two hours and contained a discussion of goals, was also confirmed by Ms Rice. Id. 41-42. Accord, Tr. at 1302-1303, where Mrs. M testifies that she participated in the Meeting.

On June 14, 2007, the CSE reconvened for the annual review and formulated an IEP on that date, a copy of which is in evidence as District's Ex. D-3. Regarding this annual review, Ms. Rice also testifies at length and the document speaks for itself in demonstrating that an appropriate program was created to meet this child's needs.

First, on page 5 of Exhibit D-3, it is noted that the outside neuropsychological evaluation dated January 19, 2007, conducted by Dr. X Ph.D. ("the X Report"), which is District's Exhibit D-11 in evidence, was one of the documents upon which this IEP is based. Accord, Tr. at 48-49, where Ms. Rice refers to the X Report as "by a very well credentialed individual" and an "excellent evaluation." Id.

Ms. Rice further states that the CSE followed up on the recommendation made in the X Report in discussing "the possibility of a school other than the public school in [this district]" Tr. at 49-50. Ms. Ryan continues, testifying that "the district said it was open to exploring that as an option. But the mother, Mrs. L, was not interested in that option." Tr. at 50. Accord, District Ex. D-3, Comments Section p. 5, Paragraph 4.

Moreover, District Ex. D-3 further states, and Ms. Rice's testimony further confirms, that "the Wilson Reading Program was again offered to the student due to his weakness in decoding." District Ex. D-3, Comments Section, Paragraph 4. Ms. Rice's testimony also confirms her belief that the District did offer "summer tutoring in Wilson at the Summer School" at this Meeting, even though the Comments Section to this IEP indicates that the District stated at this CSE Meeting that the child "is not eligible for an extended school year program based on his level of functioning." District Ex. D-3 at p. 5 Comments Section, Paragraph 6; Tr. at 50.

Ms. Rice also indicates that the number of Resource Room days in this child's program was reduced in this IEP from four days to three days so as to allow the Wilson Reading Plan to take place. Tr. at 53. Additionally, Ms. Rice testifies that this IEP Meeting lasted approximately two hours and that Mrs. M was afforded "a full opportunity to participate" in the formulation of this IEP. Id. Accord, Tr. at 1309, where Mrs. M states she participated in this meeting from start to end.

Concerning the third IEP dated September 27, 2007, which is District's Ex. D-3 in evidence, this is the Report of a Subcommittee which convened at Mrs. M's request for an IEP review after a meeting she had with Mrs. Lackey, the District's Assistant Superintendent for Pupil Services, during the Summer of 2007. Tr. at 57-58. See Ex. D-4, where the same programs outlined in the June 2007 IEP were repeated, namely Consultant Teacher Direct three times per week, Consultant Teacher Indirect once per week, and Special Class Social Studies once per week. Also, this third IEP notes that an Assistive Technology Evaluation was requested and was to be performed in the Fall of 2007. Tr. at 59; District Ex. D-4 at page 5, Comments Section, Paragraph 2.

Like the June 2007 IEP, the September 2007 IEP specifically refers again to consideration by the CSE of the X Report. Id. at p. 5; Tr. at 60. Also, Ms. Rice testified that this Meeting, like the first two IEPs for School Year 2007-2008, lasted more than two hours and had to be continued so as to allow for a discussion of goals and objectives. Tr. at 61-62.

Thereafter, the CSE again reconvened on November 9, 2007. The IEP emanating from that Meeting is District Exhibit D-5 in evidence. The X Report is once again listed among the Reports upon which this IEP is based. See, Ex. D-5 at 5[6]. And, like the two previous 2007-2008

---

6   The X Report was among the Reports listed upon which the last three IEPs for School Year 2007-2008 were based. The Report was not made available for consideration in the formulation for the first IEP.

IEPs, this IEP was formulated with the mother's full participation to meet this child's needs. See, Tr. At 66, where Ms. Rice testifies, "[T] here was definitely a thoughtful process in place and certainly the intent of all of his teachers that we provide him with the best instructional program for his learning."

In addition to the four IEPs created for this child concerning School Year 2007-2008, this hearing officer should also review the report noted above of the IST (Instructional Support Team) of November 2006, which is District's Ex. D-13 in evidence. In the IST Report, it is demonstrated that the District recommended further testing for the child in light of the mother's concern about decoding. Thus, contrary to the Parents' contention at the hearing, the District did deal with Blake's decoding issues in advance of the Parents' commissioning of the X Report. The IST Report states " (School Psychologist) reviewed the findings of this reevaluation conducted in the middle school and noted that decoding/spelling were relative weaknesses." District Ex. D-13 at p. 1. And, at this Exhibit's p. 3, it is further demonstrated that even prior to School Year 2007-2008, Wilson was offered for this child and refused by the parent and that "Circle Sheets" and testing were suggested but refused at that time by Mrs. M. Id.

Moreover, concerning the IEPs and the IST, it was demonstrated at hearing the that none of the IEPs were rejected by Mrs. M after they were promulgated until this hearing request was brought months and months later. See Tr. at 1325-1350.

2: THE IEPs MEET THE FAPE REQUIREMENTS IN THAT, AMONG OTHER THINGS, THE CHILD HAS MADE SATISFACTORY PROGRESS

In addition to the IEPs having been fashioned to create a reasonable and appropriate program for this child with more then complete participation by his parents, the child has made satisfactory progress in the program outlined by these IEPs. The legal standard regarding progress by the child is as follows: "A school district fulfills its substantive obligations under the IDEA if it provides an IEP that is likely to 'produce progress, not regression' and provides the student with opportunity greater than mere 'trivial advancement'". Cerra v. Pawling Central School District, 427 F. 3d 186,195 (2d. Cir. 2005)(quoting Walczak v. Florida Union Free School District, 142 F.3d 119, 130 (2d Cir. 1998). Objective evidence is analyzed to determine what qualifies as "generally accepted indicators of satisfactory progress", such as attainment of passing grades and advancement to a higher grade level by a mainstreamed student or test scores for a child in self-contained special education class. See Walczak, 142 F. 3d at 130. Indeed, school districts are not required to "maximize" the potential of students with disabilities, but rather ensure an "appropriate" education, "not one that provides everything that might be thought desirable by loving parents." See Rowley, supra, 48 U.S. at 213, Walczak 142 F. 3d at 132.

In Rye Neck, supra, the parents of a special needs student were seeking tuition reimbursement for placement of their child in a private school for special needs students, asserting that the child was not making proper progress under the District's IEP. The court looked at the student's successful grade promotion, IEP short-term objective accomplishments and positive teacher testimony indicating progress in essentially all of the child's courses, as well as his social development therein and determined that the IEP was adequate and accordingly awarded no reimbursement. Id. at *16. The appropriateness of the parents' unilateral placement and equitable considerations was not ruled upon by the court because the inquiry ended upon the finding that the defendant School District's IEP was appropriate. With a justifiably contrary result in Mrs. B. v. Milford Bd. of Education, 103 F.3d 1114 (2d Cir.1997), the Second Circuit did grant reimbursement upon determining, unlike here, that there was insufficient progress by the student under the IEP created for him because of the failure of the child to achieve IEP goals, the child's inability to advance to the next grade level, and the child's generally low grade scores.

Upon a review of this record, the progress of the child in this case is very much like that of the child in Rye Neck and totally dissimilar to that of the child in Milford. Blake's progress has been far more than "trivial". He has passed all required Regents exams to date and, indeed, has never failed a course. See testimony of Mrs. M, Tr. at 1417 and 1525-1526. He also has progressed from grade to grade. See District Ex. D-12, D-11 (as discussed in the X Report.); and Tr. at 1124 (testimony of Mrs. M.) See also Parents' Ex. P-F.

In addition, Ms. Rice indicates in testimony that there has been progress made by Blake in high school. Id. at 66-67, where she testifies that Blake "is increasingly becoming a more independent student, he's increasingly becoming a more involved student and I think his current grades reflect an improvement in his courses." Accord, testimony of Mrs. Abeles, Blake's English teacher, where she states that Blake "has made significant progress over the course of the year", and that she had just written a letter of recommendation for him. Tr. at 924. (emphasis added). See also Tr. at 223-224, where Ms. Manna indicates that this student "has improved" and "has improved a little each quarter" and "received a B on his last report card grade."

Substantial progress by Blake is also evidenced by, among other items in the record, the Classroom Observation Checklists, which contain observations of Blake's eighth and ninth grade courses, where he received high marks in classroom behavior and social interaction. See District Ex. D-6 and D-9 in evidence. In addition, other evidence of the child's continued progress is found in the X Report. See District Ex. D-11 at page 17, where Dr. X, the parent's witness at the hearing and whose Report is the centerpiece of the Parent's contentions, states that the child's WIAT-II test results show a reading comprehension grade equivalent of 8.5, which is very close to his actual ninth grade level at that time.

Furthermore, District's Ex. D-12 in evidence, which is a Report Card for this child for School Year 2007-2008, shows passing grades in all of this child's courses in Marking Periods 1, 2 and 3, and in School Year 2005. In addition, District's Exhibits 24 and 25 in evidence, which are statements of goals progress, show that each goal has either been "achieved," or that "some progress" or "satisfactory progress" has been made by this child on all of his measurable annual goals during School

Year 2007-2008. <u>Accord</u>, District Exhibits 29 and 30 in evidence and Tr. at 1415. (Reports of the IEP goals in 2006-2007 and 2007-2008.)

Furthermore, the Parents' contention that the CSE has failed to consider the X Report in the promulgation of the 2007-2008 IEPs could not be further from the truth. Indeed, the CSE not only gave due consideration to the X Report as soon as it was provided by the Parents to the Team, but in reality, offered private school placement as recommended by Dr. X, and the mother rejected this without explanation. <u>See</u> District Ex. D-3, IEP dated June 14, 2007, Comments Section, Paragraph 4, where it is noted that Mrs. M indicated without further explanation that private school placement "is not an option." This is also evidenced in the two other IEPs promulgated for this School Year in question. <u>See</u> <u>also</u> fn. 6 <u>supra</u>, where it is noted that the CSE specifically indicated its full consideration of the X Report in the second, third and fourth IEPs.

Thus, as soon as it was made available by the Parents, the CSE specifically followed the recommendations of the X Report. Moreover, an Independent Education Evaluation ("IEE") at District expense was never requested by the Parents and the procedures outlined in 8 N.Y.C.R.R. § 200.5(g) were not followed by the Parents to obtain an IEE.

In sum, the record amply demonstrates that despite the incessant interference by the Parents, who were accorded much more than full participation in the process, the IEPs produced by the CSE concerning the child's program in School Year 2007-2008 resulted in appropriate educational progress.

3: <u>THE IEPs ARE NOT DEFICIENT BECAUSE THEY DO NOT SPECIFY WILSON READING IN THE PROGRAM DESCRIPTION</u>

The IEPs are not legally deficient in any way under these facts because they do not specify Wilson Reading in their Program descriptions.

Perhaps most important is the clear record made at the hearing that it was the Parents who consistently rejected the Wilson methodology. See, e.g., discussion supra of each of the 2007-2008 IEPs, including the testimony of Ms. Ryan elucidating clearly that Wilson was offered at each of the four IEP Meetings convened and at the IST Meeting in November 2006 and rejected by the Parents. Accord, Tr. at 416, where Mr. Jack, the Assistant Principal who communicated regularly with Mrs. M, testifies in answer to questions as to how many times the Wilson Reading Program was offered and how many times it was rejected by the Parents: "I remember four."

It must be also be noted that the law is abundantly clear that an IEP need not specially mention a methodology, such as Wilson, in its Program Section in order for such to be considered to have been "offered" to a student. There is no requirement that a teaching methodology be set out as part of the child's program in an IEP. Therefore, the failure to list a specific teaching methodology or methodologies in the child's program on an IEP does not signify that the IEP is inappropriate.

The use of particular methodologies is in the teacher's discretion. See, Application of a Child with a Disability, Appeal No. 94-26; Application of a Child with a Disability, Appeal No. 95-15[7]; Application

---

7   In Application of a Child with a Disability, Appeal No. 95-15, the child was six years old. The child had been enrolled in an early intervention program at the age of one and a half. In September 1993, the Committee on Preschool Special Education ("the CPSE") had recommended that the child be classified as autistic and enrolled him on a ten-month basis in a center-based preschool program with small group and individual speech/language and individual occupation therapies for the 1993-1994 School Year. The parents did not accept the CSPE's recommendation for the child's placement and instead enrolled the child in the Little Miracles Preschool Program. In June 1994, the CSE recommended classification as autistic and placement in an SIE-III class on a twelve month basis for the 1994-1995 School Year. The CSE also recommended speech/language therapy in a group of no more than two children, three times per week and individual speech/language therapy twice per week. The parents again did not accept the recommendations and enrolled their son in the Eden II School for the 1994-1995 School Year. In 1994, the parents requested an impartial hearing.

The impartial hearing officer held that the school district met its burden of proving the SIE-III class was appropriate to meet the child's needs. The hearing officer also found that personnel at P.S. 37 were trained in Lovaas behavior modification and could utilize it if appropriate. The SRO then found that because the precise method

of a Child with a Disability, Appeal No. 02-022; and Application of a Child with a Disability, Appeal No. 05-053. Therefore, even if Mrs. M consented at any time to the Wilson Reading Program for her child, which it has been clearly demonstrated she did not, the CSE would not have been required to list the Wilson methodology as part of Blake's program in his IEPs.

Another important aspect of the evidence admitted at the hearing is the testimony and emails of District representatives recommending that Mrs. M urged Blake to attend "extra help" sessions after school. The evidence shows that Mrs. M did not make sure that Blake attended extra help sessions on a regular basis. Accordingly, the provision of these extra help sessions, which were part of the program offered by the District, bolsters the District's Prong One argument in that it shows another most appropriate aspect of the District recommended program for this child, which aspect was not followed by the Parents. Mrs. M by and large completely rejected extra help for Blake. See Jack Email page J-321 in evidence, where Mrs. M asks for help but cautions the District not to recommend extra help any more since this "is not the solution to this." Accord, Email J-79, where Mrs. M states: "Blake came into the high school with, granted, a negative attitude towards going to extra help."[8]

In addition, the February 12, 2007 IEP, District's Ex. D-2 in evidence, notes in its Comments Section that "the student should be encouraged to regularly attend extra help sessions provided by his teachers." The educators also consistently encouraged Mrs. M to make sure that Blake made attending extra help sessions regularly a priority. See, e.g., Tr. at 417-18, where, as noted above, Mr. Jack testified:

---

of teaching methodology to be used by a child's teacher is a method to be left to the teacher, the program recommended by the CSE was appropriate even though the IEP did not explicitly provide for use of the Lovaas behavior management technique.

8   This rejection of extra help by Mrs. M also strongly supports the District's Prong Three argument that the equities do not favor the Parents' request for reimbursement for outside Wilson reading or tutoring services because Mrs. M refused or failed to make sure that Blake regularly attended extra help sessions offered by his teachers. See also discussion infra.

[I]n every meeting including smaller meetings, not necessarily official meetings…, there was always the statement…what about extra help. And that was in email correspondence as well. Blake was invited of course to go to extra help as all students are by his teachers. A lot of the response in ninth grade was Blake can't go to extra help or Blake shouldn't go to extra help or its not going to be helpful or he prefer[s] to go to the basketball, whatever it was. There was also some reasons why extra help wasn't going to work for Blake and those responses were not really coming from Blake, but Mrs. M, speaking, I guess, on behalf of Blake.

Then, in answer to the question: "About how often would you say you encouraged Mrs. M to have Blake attend extra help sessions? Mr. Jack testified by answering: "I think between me and teachers, I'm probably going to low ball and say about 25. There had to be at least 25 times it was brought up between me and teachers. Me, myself, easily four…maybe five." Tr. at 417-18. Accord, Tr. at 302-305, testimony of Mrs. Gilley.

Accordingly, the District has satisfactorily met its burden under Rowley, Walczak and their progeny in demonstrating that a FAPE has been provided, which has resulted in more then satisfactory progress being made by the child. Therefore, the District clearly satisfies the First Prong of the Burlington/Carter test because the IEP created by the District should be found to be appropriate. Hence, all relief requested by the Parents should be denied, and the Parents' request for reimbursement of costs of tutoring, reading instruction, and the X Report should be denied in all respects.

Upon this hearing officer's finding that the IEPs are appropriate and that the District has met its burden under Burlington/Carter, the adequateness of the Parents' services obtained unilaterally and equitable considerations need not be ruled upon. See Rye Neck, supra. Nevertheless, in the alternative, the District submits herewith the following sections demonstrating no entitlement to relief by the Parents under either of the remaining prongs, even if it is found that a FAPE was not provided by the District.

B. EVEN IF IT IS FOUND THAT A FAPE WAS NOT PROVIDED BY THE DISTRICT, THE PARENTS HAVE FAILED TO DEMONSTRATE ANY LEGAL RIGHT TO REIMBURSEMENT FOR THE EVALUATION, TUTORING, OR REMEDIAL READING INSTRUCTION THEY OBTAINED UNILATERALLY

In the alternative, even if FAPE is deemed not to have been provided by the District, which is clearly not the case here, the Parents have failed to fulfill their burden to demonstrate any legal right to reimbursement for their unilaterally and privately obtained evaluation, tutoring, or remedial reading instruction.

Reimbursement is only appropriate where a FAPE was not provided for by a district and the parents demonstrate that they paid for educational expenses which should have been borne by the district from the outset. See Burlington, 471 U.S. at 370,371. (emphasis added) Therefore, merely showing that the District failed to meet its requirement to provide a FAPE is insufficient for an award of reimbursement. The services for which reimbursement is requested must be demonstrated to be appropriate and the interests of equity must favor the parents.

The Second Circuit has held: "Subject to certain limited exceptions [not relevant here], the same considerations and criteria that apply in determining whether the school district's placement is appropriate should be considered in determining the appropriateness of the parent's placement." Gagliardo v. Arlington Cent. School District., 489 F. 3d. 105, 112 (citations and internal quotation marks omitted). Thus, the Parents have the burden to demonstrate that the services they obtained for this child met his unique needs and enabled him to receive educational benefits in light of the totality of circumstances. See Id. at 112. As detailed below, no such showing has been made by the Parents.

In Application of the Board of Education of the East Ramapo

Central School District, Appeal No. 07-137 the State Review Officer ("SRO") held that tuition reimbursement from the District was not appropriate where the parents of a special needs student did not provide adequate information regarding the progress made by the child while enrolled in the parents' placement, which was a special needs school. The SRO found that the parents provided insufficient evidence to show that their placement met the unique needs of the student. The SRO further found that it was not shown by the parents that the services rendered were ones from which the child could benefit. See Appeal No. 07-137 at pp.11-12. (citing Gagliardo, 489 F. 3d. at 112; Frank G 459 F. 3d. at 363-65.)

Similarly, in Board of Education of the Ellenville Central School District, Appeal No. 96-77, the parents of a special needs student receiving home-based instruction sought tuition reimbursement, as is the case with the Parents here. The SRO denied these parents' request because he found that they had failed to demonstrate that the child's special needs were met by the services they had obtained or that the child was making sufficient progress. The SRO held that in the absence of any evidence and documentation by parents of the nature of education received by the child in the home-based instruction, there is no basis to order reimbursement. Id. (emphasis added.)

Similarly, in the instant case, nowhere in the Parent's Exhibits or in the testimony at the hearing is there any credible or cogent evidence of the adequacy and appropriateness of the home tutoring which they unilaterally provided in subject areas or in remedial reading for their child. Likewise, there is no proof presented by the Parents that either Dr. X or any of the Parents' tutors or providers of remedial reading sought any information from the District as to the learning provided in this child's day program. The Parents' submissions on these facts are nothing more than Invoices reflecting amounts paid and brief testimony on these Invoices. Tr. 1215-1220; Parents Ex. P-K. No documentation or testimony has been submitted demonstrating the quality or relevance to Blake's needs of the services provided. Having not done so, they have failed to meet their burden in order to qualify for reimbursement under applicable law.

C. THE EQUITIES DO NOT FAVOR THE PARENTS' CLAIM FOR REIMBURSEMENT OR FOR ANY RELIEF HERE

The interests of equity clearly do not in any way favor the Parents' claim for reimbursement or for any relief here. Should it be determined that an appropriate FAPE was not provided by the District, which has not been shown, and that the Parents were able to bring forward evidence of an adequate alternative education, which also has not been shown, the Third Prong of the Burlington/Carter test is not met here in that equitable considerations clearly do not favor the Parents and no relief may be granted to the Parents.

In the instant case, the interests of equity do not favor the Parents' requests for relief of any kind here. As previously detailed, Mrs. M bombarded the District with emails, continuously attempted program and teacher changes as well as retaking of tests and grade reevaluation, did not ensure that the child regularly attended extra help sessions, and many times rejected the Wilson Reading Program sought to be inserted by the District into Blake's schedule. See e.g., discussion supra. at pages 9-14. Mrs. M demonstrated no intention to work with the District in providing an appropriate educational program for the child. On the other hand, the District attempted at all times in good faith to satisfy all of the myriad, unrelenting requests of Mrs. M.

Furthermore, the Parents did not follow the procedure as spelled out in 8 N.Y.C.R.R. § 200.5(g) for having the X Report considered an Independent Educational Evaluation for which the District would be required to pay. The Parents did not demonstrate that they gave notice to the District before obtaining the X Report. Similarly, the Parents gave no demonstrated notice to the District and did not show at the hearing that they obtained any kind of District authorization for home tutoring or private reading remedial instruction. By her own admission, Mrs. M did not give any prior notice to the District of her beginning outside Wilson tutoring at the end of February 2007. Tr. at 1307-1309. Therefore, the equities clearly do not favor reimbursement to the Parents for these services.

Similarly, the Parents did not demonstrate at the hearing that they ever informed the District in writing that they were going to have Blake evaluated by Sylvan Learning Center or Huntington Learning Center, Tr. at 1354-1355, and never requested payment for these services prior to this hearing request. Tr. at 1354-1355. Thus, the Parents' claim for reimbursement for these services must be rejected in full.

Also, Mrs. M is asking for reimbursement for tutoring in math, a subject in which this child has never failed a class. See Tr. at 1359, and in biology. Id. In sum, Mrs. M is asking for reimbursement for this private tutoring even though it is questionable whether it was needed and it was not shown that Mrs. M ever asked for reimbursement from the District for Blake before she commenced these private services.

The operative legal standard should be repeated here. The District is not required to provide each and every service which a "loving parent" would desire, but is simply required to provide an appropriate education. See discussion supra. at pp. 14-15. The Parents' request that Blake's home tutoring and private remedial reading instruction be reimbursed as a result of the alleged inadequacies of the IEP is the Parents' seeking reimbursement for educational services way above and beyond that which the District is required to provide. The District need not reimburse for each and every possibly helpful program of a parents' choosing, which is exactly what is being requested by the Parents.

In addition, the testimony at the hearing clearly establishes that the actions of the Parents defeated the goals of the IDEA. "The core of the statute is the collaborative process between parents and schools, primarily through the IEP process." Schaffer, 546 U.S. at 532. As evidenced by, among other things, the massive numbers of emails sent by Mrs. M to the District concerning her child and the numerous instances of Mrs. M's refusal to permit the Wilson remedial reading in Blake's program and his participation in extra help, Mrs. M has made an insufficient attempt to work with the District in the "collaborative process" of obtaining a suitable educational program for the child.

Thus, rather than work collaboratively with the District, the hearing has clearly demonstrated that the Parents have, in effect, blocked the District from providing Wilson and other services to Blake and not cooperated in any significant aspect of this child's program. Therefore, there are no equitable considerations which justify favoring any kind of award for reimbursement to the Parents.

IV.   CONCLUSION

The District has convincingly demonstrated in detail the adequacy of the FAPE which it provided for Blake. Conversely, insufficient evidence has been provided by the Parents as to the appropriateness of the services for which reimbursement is sought. In addition, no equitable entitlement by the Parents to the reimbursement they seek has been shown and, indeed, none of the relief they seek has been demonstrated as appropriate.

Accordingly, the Parents should not be awarded reimbursement for the educational services and evaluation they obtained unilaterally for their child and no other relief should be awarded to the Parents.

Respectfully submitted,
Dated: November 7, 2008, Attorneys for School District

APPENDIX B
DECISION OF "IMPARTIAL" HEARING OFFICER (11/22/08)

From: <u>Dr. Orange</u>

Date: November 22, 2008

In the Matter of a Proceeding Brought by Parents on Behalf of Their Son, Pursuant to Part 200 of the Regulations of the Commissioner of Education, Petitioners

-and-

The School District, Respondent

<u>**APPEARANCES:**</u>

Law Office of Andrew K. Carter, Attorneys for Petitioner, Parent, Andrew Carter, Esquire

-and-

Attorneys for Respondent, School District, Mr. Waters, Esquire/ Mrs. Rock, Esquire

On February 28, 2008, the School District (District) Board of Education appointed an Impartial Hearing Officer for a due process hearing requested by petitioners, the parents, on behalf of their son (DOB: 6/92, Case Identifier: 32668). In a letter dated February 12,

2008, (received by District February 20, 2008) the parents notified the District of their intent through hearing to seek:

- Annulment of the current IEP

- Provision of a appropriate IEP (with consideration of the independently obtained Neuropsychological report)

- Provision of an assistive technology evaluation and implementation of recommendations and goals to address the recommendations

- Provision of the Wilson Reading Program, by an experienced qualified Level II or trainer, of the Parents choosing, for a minimum of one (1 hour daily) at the convenience of the family

- Provision of extended school day academic intervention services to remediate all content areas (The District shall pay for the continuation of the current tutor's services.)

- Provision of an intensive extended school year reading program of the Parent's choosing

- Reimbursement for the reading instruction that the Parents paid for privately

- Reimbursement for the academic tutoring that the Parents paid for privately

- Reimbursement for the independent neuropsychological evaluation that the Parents paid for privately

- Payment of the Parent's attorney fees and expenses associated with representation in this matter

- Development of an appropriate plan of transition that includes goals and objectives and services designed to assist the student in achieving those goals and objectives

- Provision of any further relief that the Hearing Officer deems just and proper[9]

---

9   Ex. PA Parent's Demand for Due Process Hearing

Through their attorney, the parents agreed to waive the resolution session, therefore, a prehearing telephone conference between the Hearing Officer, the attorney for the parents and attorney for the District was scheduled for March 18, 2008, to clarify hearing issues, establish hearing date(s) and identify other administrative matters. The written summary of the prehearing conference[10] noted that both parties were able to move forward with the hearing on April 28, 2008 at the School District offices.

The initial hearing date changed, agreed to by all parties, took place on May 1, 2008 and continued with eight (8) additional hearing dates until, October 7, 2008. Extensions of the required timeline, due to illness, surgery, personal family issues, scheduling of witnesses and extensive testimony, were requested and granted by the Hearing Officer. Although this hearing was very protracted, there was no objection to extension by either party, therefore, the compliance date for the record close and decision due dates were extended on several occasions. Post Hearing <u>Memoranda of Law</u> were received from the attorney for the District and the Attorney for the Parent on November 12th and November 13th, 2008, respectively. The Hearing Decision is rendered on November 22, 2008.

FINDINGS OF FACT

At the initiation of the hearing challenging the 2007-2008 10th Grade IEP, the student, a male, fifteen year-eleven month old, resided in the (District) with his parents and siblings. The student attended the District schools since elementary school and there is no dispute of his classification as a student with a learning disability.

The student first received special education services in the elementary school. During the 9th grade school year at the high school, the student continued to receive special education services, along with the program modification of preferential seating and test accommodations.[11] The

---

10 Ex. IHO 1
11 Ex. D 2

CSE met on February 12, 2007 for a revision of the existing 9th grade IEP. As an outcome of the February 12, 2007 CSE meeting, the student's services were increased at the request of the Parent, believing the student required a "more restrictive and supportive program." The student was moved from a mainstream Social Studies class to a more restrictive special education Social Studies class; even though the comments reveal that, the class profile indicated that the other students were "indeed at a lower functioning level…." The student's program was further modified to include the more restrictive special education English. IEP comments also noted that District personnel recommended the Wilson Reading Program (a structured phonic based program), but there was concern as to whether the student's schedule would accommodate participation this year (2006-2007). The special education administrator and Parent agreed that scheduling would be difficult and didn't believe it would be practical at this time. An administrator at the meeting noted that the student didn't qualify for the program (Wilson) but that the District would "allow …his participation next year."[12]

An independent neuropsychological evaluation (IEE) initiated by the parent, was completed on January 19, 2007 and resulted in a diagnosis of Developmental Dyslexia (ICD Code 784.61) and Reading Disorder (DSM-IV-TR Code 315.00).[13] Although discussed at the February CSE meeting, based on Parent's reporting of the findings, the written evaluation report was shared with the District at sometime following the February 14, 2007 CSE meeting.

The CSE and CSE subcommittees met three subsequent times to draft an IEP[14] for the 2007-2008 school year. The parent participated in the meetings and spoke with District staff both before and after meetings. The Annual Review CSE first meeting to plan the 10th Grade 2007-2008 year, took place on June 14, 2007; all required members were present, including a "friend of the family."[15] As a result of that meeting,

---

12   Id. p.4
13   E. D 11
14   Ex. D 3,4,5
15   Ex. D 3; Person identified at hearing as an advocate (T pp.939-1040)

recommendations were that the student continue in a special education Social Studies class and receive both direct and indirect consultant teacher services to support the general education courses. The Special Education Chairperson testified, "we reduced the resource room form five days to consultant teacher direct which we basically use when we are using support service for three hours or less. And the reason why we did that was our plan would be that he would participate in the Wilson reading program the other three days." [16] The student's IEP noted the accommodations of books-on-tape, check for understanding and preferential seating and test accommodations including extended time (1.5), special location, directions read and explained, tests read (except Reading Comprehension), record short answers and monitoring of Scantron test answers ("bubble sheet" responses read electronically). The comments section of the IEP noted that the CSE reviewed the private evaluation[17] submitted by the parents in consideration of the student's achievement, performance and learning characteristics. The IEP comments further indicate that the Wilson Program was discussed, stating the difficulty with scheduling (Wilson) last year (IEP 2006-07) and further that "his mother stated that she did not want to include it (Wilson) at that time."[18] Based on recommendations of the private evaluation, the CSE participants discussed a private day school placement, which was "not considered and option" by the parent.[19] Comments indicate that the CSE recommended that the student's program for the 2007-08 school year, 10th Grade at the High School, would include self-contained Social Studies, an Intensive Earth Science, American Sign Language (ASL- to meet the Foreign Language requirement), a TV Production class, Sequential Math 2, and a general education English class co-taught by a regular and special educator. Further, indicated in the Comments section, Wilson Reading was considered by the CSE, "due to the student's weakness in decoding." The Special Education Chairperson testified that the parent requested summer tutoring in

---

16   Tr. p. 53

17   Ex. D 11 – Private Neuropsychological Evaluation (1/19/2007)

18   Ex. D 3, p.5 ("that time" meaning February 2007.)

19   Id.

the Wilson Program and that "after the meeting the District did offer summer tutoring in Wilson at the Summer School."[20] In addition, the student was to receive Consultant Teacher services to help with the student's organizational issues. The mother requested that the Consultant Teacher not be used for homework completion. The Chairperson offered a "Franklin Speller," which the parent did not think he would use. The student's Level I Vocational Assessment was discussed and the parent requested a copy of the report indicating that she hadn't received it. In addition, an Assistive Technology evaluation was requested by the parent to be scheduled in the fall of 2007. Comments indicated that the parent requested that the District pay for the Wilson tutoring that her son had been receiving outside of school for school year (2006-07) and also for summer tutoring (summer 2007). The CSE Chairperson informed the parent that based on the student's level of functioning; he was not eligible for an extended school year program.[21]

The purpose of the CSE meeting held on September 9, 2007 at Parent request was to review the role of the Resource Room teacher (Consultant Teacher), and concerns about the restriction on homework completion in the Resource Room (Consultant Teacher Direct). Comments note that the student made a request to the teacher that he be allowed to work on homework and the teacher agreed that a review of homework could develop appropriate strategies. It was agreed by the Committee, that the restriction be lifted, on the condition that the Resource Room not be used as a study hall. Comments also noted that the parent had met with the Assistant Superintendent and other special education personnel over the summer. Due to a lack of time, IEP goals were not modified.[22] No discussion is noted in the CSE comments for this meeting about the Student Schedule[23] dated 8/22/2007. The parent received the schedule and noted on it "rec 8/29/07 No PE!!". This Student Schedule at Period 8 had Wilson Reading, Marking Period 1,2,3 and 4, Days 1,3,5 with

---

20   Tr. p. 50 (The Summer School is a separate site in the District that offers a 12 month program.)
21   Ex. D 3, p.5
22   Ex. D 4
23   Ex. G1

a room and teacher assigned. The record did not reflect any comment about why this course (Wilson) was ever implemented.

An additional review of the IEP took place on November 9, 2007 and changed Consultant Teacher Direct and Indirect services to Resource Room services, five days out of a six day cycle - 44 minutes.[24] Because Wilson was not implemented, Resource Room services were increased on the IEP. The Special Education Chairperson testified, "...at this time there was a more definitive decision that [the student] would not participate in the Wilson program. nd we changed the IEP to reflect the fact that he was receiving more than three hours of direct service in the resource room. So it was no longer three days consultant teacher but five days."[25] This change increased the student's direct services by 88 minutes per week. As Parent continued to express concern about the student's grades being adversely affected by incorrect spelling and grammar in content area courses, CSE members recommended the student's continued use of a word processor.

PETITIONER ARGUMENT

1. *A Program is only offered to a parent when it is included on an IEP.*

The parents allege failure of the District to provide a free appropriate education (FAPE), by declining to offer the student specifically designed instruction in reading or math, by failing to accurately describe his present levels of performance in his IEP, and failing to provide resource room on a daily basis. The parents further allege the District's failure to consider the privately obtained neuropsychological evaluation report, failure to conduct the recommended assistive technology evaluation in a timely fashion, failure to provide appropriate classroom and testing accommodations, failure to implement an appropriate transition plan, failure to provide appropriate measurable annual goals and failure to provide summer programming. The parents requested, inter alia,

    1: Annulment of the current IEP

---

24   Ex. D 5 p.1
25   Tr. p. 63

2: Provision of a appropriate IEP with consideration of the independently obtained Neuropsychological report and the Assistive Technology evaluation. The IEP shall address the student's academic, social, emotional and physical management needs. Current, accurate PLEPs[26] (including the diagnosis of dyslexia and other diagnoses as indicated in the evaluation (Ex. D11) shall be included. Necessary methodologies, appropriate, measurable goals to address the needs indicated, and an appropriate transition plan shall be developed and reflected on the IEP.

3: Provision of an assistive technology evaluation and implementation of recommendations and goals to address the recommendations.

4: Provision of the Wilson Reading Program, by an experienced qualified Level II or trainer, of the Parents choosing, for a minimum of one (1 hour daily) at the convenience of the family.

5: Provision of extended school day academic intervention services to remediate all content areas. The District shall pay for the continuation of the current tutor's services.

6: Provision of an intensive extended school year reading program of the Parent's choosing

7: Reimbursement for the reading instruction that the Parents paid for privately

8: Reimbursement for the academic tutoring that the Parents paid for privately

9: Reimbursement for the independent neuropsychological evaluation that the Parents paid for privately.

10: Development of an appropriate plan of transition that

---

26   PLEP – Present Level Educational Performance

includes goals and objectives and services designed to assist the student in achieving those goals and objectives. [27]

Petitioner first argues that a program is only "offered to a parent when it is included on an IEP."[28] Petitioner refutes the District argument that they had "offered" or "recommended" the Wilson Reading Program as a part of the students "program" which was rejected by the parents on several occasions. Petitioner asserts federal courts have agreed that a school district only offers programs that are contained within a written, finalized IEP. Citing *Knable v. Bexley City School Dist.*, 238F.3d 755, 768-69, 150 Ed. law Rep. 628(6th Cir. 2001); *Union School Dist. v. Smith*, 15 F.3d 1519,1526,89 Ed Law Rep. 44 (9th Cir. 1994); *A.K. v Alexandria City School Bd.*, 484 F.3d.672, 680-81, 219Ed. Law Rep. 398 (4th Cir. 2007); *Systema v. Academy School Dist. No. 20*, 538 F.3d 1306, 1315-16, 236 Ed. law Rep.94 (10th Cir.2008),[29] petitioner argues that the hearing officer must limit the evaluation of a school district's proposed IEP to the terms of the document itself, as presented in writing to the parents. Further citing the Ninth Circuits' emphasis that the district does not "escape its obligation under the IDEA to offer formally an appropriate educational placement by arguing that a disabled child's parents expressed unwillingness to accept that placement."[30] Continuing the argument that the "...formal, written offer creates a clear record that will do much to eliminate trouble-some factual disputes many years later about when placements were offered, what placements were offered, and what additional educational assistance was offered to supplement a placement, if any."[31] This argument is further supported by petitioners assertion that the "Tenth Circuit rejected the school district's argument ("that the court should consider both the written IEP as well as subsequent offers") and concluded that 'the statutory definition of an IEP ...command[s] that the courts must focus the inquiry on the draft

---

27   Parents Closing Brief pp 3-4
28   Id. p.6
29   Parent's Closing Brief p.6
30   Id.
31   Id. (from 20 U.S.C. §1415(b)(1)(E))

IEP as written.'"[32] Petitioner concludes that the "absence of the Wilson program on the IEP dooms the IEP to inappropriateness."[33]

2. *Student requires a systematic, individualized phonics program to receive a FAPE.*

Petitioner asserts that the independent evaluation stressed the need for reading intervention to focus on "making...knowledge and application of phonics to word decoding more accurate as well as automatic." The report further emphasized that the focus of the intervention should be to "enhance the student's basic decoding skills, as well as increase his automaticity when reading by building his store of sight words." The evaluation report recommended the use of a "systematic, phonologically-based, individualized reading program..." done "sensitively so as not to embarrass [the student]." (See Ex. D11) Petitioner asserts that although the District "trumpets its willingness to offer a Wilson program (which nonetheless was not offered), it insisted on a *group* program despite the recommendation of the [the independent evaluator] and apparent committee consensus the [student] needed an *individual* program. Concluding, the petitioner reasserts that the District's "failure to offer such a program *on the [student's] IEP* thus denies him FAPE." [34]

3. *The annual goals in reading are not appropriate.*

Petitioner concludes that the annual goals in reading were well below the student's level of achievement and did not meet the standard set forth in the Part 200 regulations.[35] Petitioner sets forth that the reading goals on the IEP did not reflect the student's current needs, as he "already knew [them] without any teaching" and other IEP goals were "so vague as to be meaningless," and therefore "do not provide FAPE."[36]

4. *The IEP does not offer an appropriate transition plan.*

---

32   Id. p.7 (from 538 F.3d. at 1315)

33   Id.

34   Id. p. 8

35   8 NYCRR 200.49(d)(2)(iii)

36   Parents Closing Brief p. 11

Petitioner asserts that although the November 2007-08 IEP provides only "boilerplate language" and offers only that "[t]he student intends to pursue a college education," and lists only five activities in the IEP, listed as the "Coordinated Set of Transition Activities." [37] Petitioner concludes that these activities are not individualized "rendering the whole section devoid of meaningful content," claiming that nothing provides for "assisting [the student] in his post-secondary goal, college;" for "assistance in choosing schools, obtaining applications, completing applications, or ensuring that [the student] will receive support under section 504 of the Rehabilitation Act while attending college." Petitioner contends, "[a]s such, the transition plan is inadequate, and denies [the student] a FAPE."[38]

5. *The District's attacks on the parents and the student are irrelevant.*

Petitioner states that the District "devoted an exorbitant amount of hearing time exploring the number of emails sent by the parent to district staff, and complaining that [the student] did not skip basketball practice to seek optional after-school help with his classes." Petitioner asserts that the District "carries the burden of developing an appropriate program irrespective of parental conduct." Citing *Union School Dist. v Smith, supra, 15F3d at 1526,* Petitioner emphasizes that a District "cannot escape its obligation under IDEA to offer formally an appropriate educational placement by arguing that a disabled child's parents expressed unwillingness to accept that placement."[39]

6. *The IHO should award reimbursement for tutoring services obtained by the parent.*

Petitioner contends that the District "refused to provide specialized reading services for [the student]'" and therefore, "the parents felt forced to obtain those services themselves." Asserting that the "district did not provide Wilson; the parent cannot be faulted for obtaining Wilson services on her own." Further stating, "the record clearly shows that the District refused to provide Wilson in a manner that would allow

---

37   Ex. P B p. 4/Ex. D 5
38   Parents Closing Brief p. 13
39   Id. pp.13-14

[the student] to continue resource room and to complete his foreign language (ASL) requirement for graduation." Additionally Petitioner contends, that [the student] "required extra help because the District failed to remediate his reading problems."[40]

7. *The school district should reimburse the parents for the [independent] evaluation.*

Petitioner asserts, "[i]f a parent disagrees with an evaluation obtained by the school district, the parent has a right to obtain an independent evaluation at public expense." Contending that the District did not initiate "hearing to prove that its' psychological evaluation… was appropriate," therefore, "the school district should thus be required to reimburse for the [independent] evaluation."[41] The Petitioner seeks the following relief:

1: An order annulling the November 2007 IEP;

2: Reimbursement for the tutoring services obtained by the parents

3: A finding that the school district denied [the student] a FAPE during the 2007-08 school year;

4: Additional services, in the form of individualized Wilson reading services, to compensate for deprivation of instruction;

5: Reimbursement for [independent] evaluation and report;

6: An order directing the CSE to reconvene following the AT evaluation to develop an appropriate program, with updated present levels of performance, meaningful and measurable annual goals correlating to the Wilson Reading Program, and an appropriate individualized transition plan;

7: Such further relief as the hearing officer deems appropriate.

---

40   Id. pp. 14-15
41   Id. pp 15-16

RESPONDENT ARGUMENT

Respondent (District) alleges that none of the Plaintiff's demands for relief concerning the 2007-08 school year were substantiated at the hearing. Further noting that there has been "no allegation by the parents that any of the teams, in the Committee on Special Education (CSE) meetings, out of which the IEPs emanated, were not properly constituted or that the Parent's participation in the CSE process was in any way denied."[42] In addition, Respondent notes that by "stipulation of counsel on the last hearing date (10/7/2008)," the complaint concerning transition planning for 2007-08 was waived by the Parents.[43] Respondent further asserts that the complaint relating to the Assistive Technology evaluation has been "largely, if not completely, mooted by the provision of such evaluation (Assistive Technology Evaluation ñ 2/15/08).[44]

Statement of Applicable Law and Facts Proven at Hearing:

"The legal standard governing the Parents' requests for reimbursement of the costs of tutoring, remedial reading services, and of a private evaluation is set forth in *School Committee of Burlington v. Dept. of Education, 471 U.S. 359 (1985)* and *Florence County School District Four v. Carter, 510 U.S. 7(1993).* Under the three-part test established by the United States Supreme Court in Burlington/Carter: "[a] board of education may be required to reimburse parents for their expenditures for the private educational services obtained for a student by his or her parents if (1) the services offered by the board of education were inadequate or inappropriate, and (2) the services selected by the parents were appropriate, and (3) equitable considerations support the parents' claim." Respondent claims that the Parents fail on each prong of the above test, they may be awarded no relief."[45]

Respondent acknowledges that under New York Education Law § 4404, the District bears the "burden of proving the adequacy and appropriateness of the educational programs it has provided...." Further

---

42   Respondent Post-Hearing Memorandum of Law pp. 2-3
43   Tr. pp.1547-8
44   Ex. D 20
45   Respondent Post-Hearing Memorandum of Law pp. 3-4

District notes, that the Parent has the "burden of persuasion as to the Parents' selected educational programs' adequacy and appropriateness."[46] District contends that the IEPs in evidence[47] demonstrate that a "free and appropriate public education ("FAPE") was provided." In addition, District states that Parents "failed to demonstrate the appropriateness of the private services for which they seek reimbursement and it was shown at hearing that equitable considerations further call for the full rejection of the Parents' claims."[48]

A. A FAPE has been provided by the CSE in the four IEPs promulgated for school year 2007-2008. Which IEPs were tailored to meet the child's individual needs and resulted in the child's satisfactory progress.

Citing *Board of Education of Hendrick Hudson Central School District v. Rowley, 458 U.S. 176 (1982),* District contends compliance with provision of an IEP "reasonably calculated to enable the child to receive educational benefits." Further District asserts that the IEPs did not have any procedural defects in their promulgation and contained all required components. The District contends that it has in "no way failed to deliver a FAPE to this child, and has not impeded the child's right to one." "Likewise, the District did in no conceivable way impede the Parents' opportunity to participate." District asserts that the Parent in many instances "attempted to lead the District in the management of [the student's] studies and curriculum...." The District maintains that they demonstrated a "clear-cut provision of FAPE" by accepting the recommendations of the independent evaluation and recommending that the Wilson Program be inserted into the child's program, and therefore, cannot "be forced to pay for Wilson remedial instruction or home tutoring...."[49]

1. *These IEPs were fashioned to create a reasonable and appropriate program*

---

46   Id. p.4
47   Ex D 2,3,4,5
48   Respondent Post-Hearing Memorandum of Law p. 4
49   Id. pp. 6-9

tailored to meet the child's needs with more then complete participation by the parents.

District contends that each of the four CSE meetings:

- were conducted with "more than complete participation by the Parents;"

- "more than met the statutory requirements;" and,

- were "tailored to meet [the student's] individual needs." [50]

The District notes that at an Instructional Support Meeting, held prior to the February 14, 2007 CSE meeting, there was a discussion regarding implementing the Wilson Reading Program. At the CSE meeting, held on the above date, the Chairperson testified at hearing "although it (Wilson) was offered, it was discussed that ...he could choose to take it at some later date....."[51] District contends that at the June 14, 2007 CSE Annual Review Meeting -for School Year 2007-2008, "an appropriate program was created to meet this child's needs."[52] The independent evaluation was one of the documents upon which the IEP was based. The Chairperson acknowledged the report as an "excellent evaluation" by a "very well credentialed individual."[53] District asserts that testimony and IEP Comments sections substantiate that the District offered, "summer tutoring in Wilson", even though the student "is not eligible for an extended school year program based on his level of functioning."[54] Further, the District notes the Chairperson testified that the "number of Resource Room days in this child's program was reduced in this IEP from five days to three days so as to allow the Wilson Reading Program to take place the other three days."[55]

District states that the third CSE meeting was held, September 27, 2007, at the request of the Parent, following a summer meeting with the new Assistant Superintendent. A subsequent IEP was generated that

---

50 Id. pp. 10-11

51 Tr. p. 40

52 Respondent Post-Hearing Memorandum of Law p. 12

53 Tr. p. 48-49

54 Respondent Post-Hearing Memorandum of Law p. 12

55 Id. p. 12, Tr. p.53

continued the program, as it was developed in June, and added a request for an Assistive Technology evaluation to be completed in the fall 2007. As with preceding meetings, District asserts that, this meeting lasted over two hours. On November 9, 2007, another CSE meeting was held and an IEP formulated "with the mother's full participation. ..." District states that the independent evaluation was again "listed among the reports upon which this IEP is based." The Chairperson testified, "there was definitely a thoughtful process in place and certainly the intent of all if his teachers that we provide him with the best instructional program for his learning." District argues that none of IEPs were "rejected by [the mother] after they were promulgated until this hearing request was brought months and months later."[56]

2. The IEPs meet the FAPE requirements in that, among other things, the child has made satisfactory progress.

District asserts that the student "has made satisfactory progress in the program outlined by these IEPs."[57] The District citing *Cerra v. Pawling Central School District, 427 F3d. 186, 195 (2d. Cir. 2005)* (Quoting Walzak v. Florida union Free School District, 142 F. 3d 119, 130 (2d. Cir 1998), notes "[a] school district fulfills its substantive obligations under the IDEA if it provides an IEP that is likely to 'produce progress, not regression' and provides the student with opportunity greater than mere 'trivial advancement.'"[58] District further stating that generally accepted indicators of satisfactory progress is "attainment of passing grades and advancement to a higher grade level by a mainstreamed student...and that districts are not "required to 'maximize' the potential of students with disabilities, but rather ensure an 'appropriate' education,' not one that provides everything that might be thought desirable by loving parents." (See Rowley, Supra, 48 U.S. at 213, Walczak 142 F3d. at 132)[59] District asserts that the student has made far more than trivial progress in that he has passed all required Regents exams to date and has never

---

56   Id. p. 13, Tr. p.66
57   Id. p. 14
58   Id. p. 14
59   Id. pp. 14-15

failed a course, progressing from grade to grade. District contends that even the independent evaluation done in February 2007 reports the student's "WIAT-II test results show a reading comprehension of 8.5, which is very close to his actual ninth grade level at that time."[60]

The District asserts that the Parents' contention that the independent evaluation report was not considered in the "promulgation of the 2007-2008 IEPs could not be further from the truth," stating that there was a discussion at the June 14, 2007 CSE of a private high school placement as recommended in the report. District contends that consideration was given to recommendations of the report in each of three meetings following receipt of the report, Parents never requested an Independent Education Evaluation (IEE) at District expense, and "procedures outlined in 8 N.Y.C.R.R. § 200.5(g) were not followed by the Parents to obtain and IEE." District concludes that the "IEPs produced by the CSE concerning the child's program for the School Year 2007-2008 resulted in appropriate educational progress."[61]

3. The IEPs are not deficient because they do not specify Wilson Reading in the program description.

"District states that the IEPs are not legally deficient... because they do not specify Wilson Reading in their Program descriptions." The District points to testimony by the Supervisor of Special Education, elucidating clearly that Wilson was offered, at each of the four IEP Meetings convened and at the IST Meeting (November 29, 2006),[62] and rejected by the Parents. The District further supports this claim with the testimony of the Assistant Principal in his testimony about the number of times that the Wilson program was offered at a CSE meeting. [63] An additional District argument is that particular methodologies are the teacher's discretion. (See Application of a Child with a Disability, Appeal No. 94-26; Application of a Child with a Disability, Appeal

---

60   Id. p. 16
61   Id. p 17
62   Ex. D 13
63   Respondent Post-Hearing Memorandum of Law pp18-20, Tr. 36-38 and
416

No. 95-15; Application of a Child with a Disability, No. 02-022; and Application of a Child with a Disability, Appeal No. 05-053). District contends that the "failure to list a specific teaching methodology or methodologies in the child's program on an IEP does not signify that the IEP is inappropriate," and even if the Parent had "consented at any time to the Wilson Reading Program … the CSE would not have been required to list the Wilson methodology as part of [the students] program on his IEP."[64]

The District asserts that it has "satisfactorily met its burden under *Rowley, Walczak* and their progeny in demonstrating that a FAPE has been provided, which has resulted in more than satisfactory progress being made by the child," and therefore, that it "clearly satisfies the First Prong of the *Burlington/Carter* test because the IEP created by the District should be found to be appropriate."[65]

B. *Even if it is found that a FAPE was not provided by the District, the parents have failed to demonstrate any legal right to reimbursement for the evaluation, tutoring, or remedial reading instruction they obtained unilaterally.*

The District asserts that "even if FAPE is deemed not to have been provided by the District …the Parents have failed to fulfill their burden to demonstrate any legal right to reimbursement for their unilaterally and privately obtained evaluation, tutoring, or remedial reading instruction." Arguing that "[r]eimbursement is only appropriate,"…"where a FAPE was not provided for by a district and the parents demonstrate that they paid for educational expenses which the district should have been borne by the district from the outset." (See *Burlington*, 471 U.S. at 370, 371) The District further argues, that the Second Circuit has held that, "… the same considerations and criteria that apply to determining whether the school district's placement is appropriate should be considered in determining the appropriateness of the parent's placement." (Gagliardo

---

64   Id. pp.18-19
65   Id. p. 20

v. Arlington Cent. School District, 489 F 3d. 105, 112) District argues that the Parents have made no showing that the services they obtained for this child met his unique needs and enabled him to receive educational benefits...." In the instant case the District asserts that "nowhere in the Parent's Exhibits or in the testimony at the hearing is there any credible or cogent evidence of the adequacy and appropriateness of the home tutoring ...unilaterally provided in subject areas or in remedial reading....The District further states that there is "no proof that the independent evaluator or any of the tutors or providers ...sought any information from the District." The Parents provided the District only with invoices reflecting amounts paid and therefore have "failed to meet their burden to qualify for reimbursement..."[66]

C. *The equities do not favor the Parent's claim for reimbursement or for any relief here.*

District asserts that the Third prong of the *Burlington/Carter* test is not met here "in that equitable considerations clearly do not favor the Parents and no relief may be granted to the Parents." District contends that the Parents many times rejected Wilson Reading inserted into the student's schedule, did not follow procedure in 8 N.Y.C.R.R. § 200.5(g) for obtaining an IEE, and failed to give notice or gain authorization regarding home tutoring or private reading remedial instruction and therefore, "the equities do not favor reimbursement to the Parents for these services." District concludes that the "adequacy of the FAPE"... and "insufficient evidence by the Parents as to the appropriateness of the services for which reimbursement is sought," "no equitable entitlement ...has been shown and ...none of the relief they seek has been demonstrated as appropriate." [67]

---

66   Id. pp. 21-22
67   Id. PP 23-25

ISSUES AND CONCLUSIONS OF LAW

1. Transition Plan

The Hearing Officer concurs with Respondent (District) that issue #11, the development of an appropriate plan of transition, was withdrawn as an issue of the 2007-2008 IEP and therefore, there will not be consideration of this issue by the Hearing Officer. [68]

2. Free Appropriate Public Education

From the record in this Hearing, I find that the CSE has recommended an appropriate program for the student in the least restrict environment. The District met the FAPE requirements in that, among other things, the student "has made satisfactory progress in the program outlined by these IEPs." The District citing *Cerra v. Pawling Central School District, 427 F3d. 186, 195 (2d. Cir. 2005)* (Quoting Walzak v. Florida union Free School District, 142 F. 3d 119, 130 (2d. Cir 1998), notes "[a] school district fulfills its substantive obligations under the IDEA if it provides an IEP that is likely to 'produce progress, not regression' and provides the student with opportunity greater than mere 'trivial advancement.'" The districts are not "required to 'maximize' the potential of students with disabilities, but rather ensure an 'appropriate' education, not one that provides everything that might be thought desirable by loving parents." (See Rowley, Supra, 48 U.S. at 213, Walczak 142 F3d. at 132)

The record demonstrates that the student has made far more than trivial progress in that he has passed all required Regents examinations to date and has never failed a course, progressing from grade to grade with 6.5 credits on his high school transcript at the end of ninth (9th) grade, 2006-07 school year.[69] The record further supports that the IEPs produced by the District's CSEs concerning the student's program for the School Year 2007-2008 demonstrated a sincere interest in planning and implementing a program directed at attainment of appropriate educational progress, through the District's willingness to review the

---

68   Tr. p. 1547
69   Ex. D12

developed IEP in two additional meetings and changing the student's program to ensure the additional support services sought by the Parent. It was asserted that there was no offer of the Wilson Reading Program in those IEPs presented in writing to the Parent. One cannot dissect the IEP, asserting that only what is written under a particular section, is the "IEP" and when written under another section of the IEP is not a part of the IEP. Therefore, I assert that the IEP is the total written document presented to the parent under the title of Individualized Educational Program, and includes all sections, including the "Comments Sections" that document the activities, discussion and intent of the Committee Members of the CSE, including the parent when present. (Note: IEPs are numbered for example, page 3 of 7, etc.) The Parent was present at all lengthy CSE meetings, had ample opportunity to participate, had an opportunity to review the written documents, and did not challenge or ask for modification of the information set forth in the Comments Section of any of the IEPs, except in this hearing several months after the last IEP. When the parent thought the IEP required review, the review was held. (Note: September and November CSE meetings.)There has been no challenge by the Parent to the Wilson Reading Program as an effective program to address the student's deficiencies that were noted in the independent evaluation. The record also supports the conclusion that the student has had the opportunity to receive a District implemented Wilson Reading Program, both in the summer between 9th and 10th grades, and during the 9th and 10th school years.[70] Further even though the Parent refused to accept the summer Wilson program offered at the Summer School, the consultant who performed the IEE noted that while the student "would likely prefer to have a relaxed summer focused on friends and basketball, the skills he might acquire during such a summer program would serve him well for the rest of his high school career and beyond."[71] The IEP comments and transcript document that the student was also encouraged to participate in additional support in subject areas by means of regularly scheduled "extra help" sessions provided by the

---

70   Ex. D 2, 3, 4, 5; P G1
71   Ex. D11 p.14

subject area teachers. There has never been a dispute about the student's intellectual ability or continued classification of Learning Disability and the more recent discrete diagnosis of "developmental dyslexia, reading disorder"[72] was embraced by the CSE as more descriptive of the student's specific types of learning disability.

Agreeing with the Parent, I find that the IEP Annual Goals for 2007-08, in reading were deficient, "well below [the student's] level of achievement,"[73] and did not accurately reflect the student's needs and abilities. While I do not find the goals so vague as to be meaningless, they certainly should have been reviewed in either of the September or November CSE meetings, to reflect the more current evaluative material and the student's actual functional level. I believe however, that not implementing the reading program (Wilson) on the student's schedule for September, may have allowed these goals to be considered "null." Nevertheless, Annual Goals should have been reviewed. The IEP (D3-June 14, 2007) was also deficient in that it did not include a "coordinated set of transition activities, however, this was remedied in the September 27, 2007 IEP (D4) which did contain the "Coordinated Set of Transition Activities."[74] Therefore, I do not find that these procedural errors impeded the student's right to a FAPE, significantly impeded the parents' opportunity to participate in the decision making process surrounding the provision of FAPE to their son, or caused deprivation of educational benefits. "FAPE mandated by federal law must include special education and related services tailored to meet the *unique needs of a particular child*,[75] (Italics mine) and must be reasonably calculated to enable the child to receive educational benefits."[76] In this instance, it is determined that the District has provided a FAPE to the student.

---

72   Id. p. 12
73   Parent Closing Brief p. 11
74   Ex. D4 p.4
75   20 U.S.C.§ 1401(a)(18)
76   Board of Education of Hendrick Hudson C.S.D. v. Rowley, 458 U.S. 176,207 [1982]

CONCLUSION

A review of the IEPs submitted into evidence and testimony provided during hearing, documented that the District provided a Free Appropriate Education Program to the student. The District developed an appropriate IEP from which the student could receive educational benefit. During the development process, with the Parent was present at each of the CSE meetings, there was consideration of evaluative data, including the independent education evaluation (together with the student's diagnosis of dyslexia/reading disorder); review of student progress and present functional levels; deliberation about placement in a "private day school" and/or other less restrictive options; test modifications; transition considerations; assistive technology consideration; and, the Wilson Reading Program. The District clearly has the obligation of balancing the education of the child in the least restrictive environment with the requirement that they receive an appropriate education.[77] An appropriate program begins with an Individualized Education Plan which accurately reflects the results of evaluations to identify the student's needs, provides for the use of appropriate special education services to address those needs and establishes annual goals which are related to the area of the student's educational deficits.[78] Arguing that the "...Second Circuit in *Walczak* also cites to a Circuit Court decision of Supreme Court Justice Ruth Bader Ginsburg which held that because public resources are not infinite, Federal Law does not secure the best education money can buy; it calls upon government, more modestly, to provide an appropriate education for each [disabled] child." [79]

The District's educational program for the student for 2007-2008 school year is adequate as it is reasonably calculated to confer some educational benefits and provide the student with a free appropriate

---

77   Briggs v. Bd. of Ed. of the State of Connecticut, 882 F. 2d 688 [2d Cir., 1989]

78   Application of a Child with a Disability, Appeal No. 93-9;

Application of a Child with a Disability, Appeal No. 93-12

79   Lunceford v. District of Columbia Bd. of Educ, 745 F.2d 1577, 1583 [D.C. C.Cir. 1984

public education that would allow "access to specialized instruction and related services which are individually designed to provide educational benefit to the handicapped child."[80]

As the IEP was reasonably calculated to confer educational benefit and provide the student with a free appropriate public education in the least restrictive environment, reimbursement is not warranted. Reimbursement is warranted only where, after the hearing, it is determined that the services offered by the school district are inadequate or inappropriate, the services selected by the parents are appropriate and equitable considerations support the parents' claim. Through this record, the Parent did not meet the obligation to support that the services they unilaterally offered to their son met his unique needs and enabled him to receive educational benefits. The record did not reflect any written reports or testimony of the teachers/tutors/organizaions who provided the unilaterally offered services to the student, nor did they consult with or make recommendations to District personnel. "IDEA provides that a local school district is not required to pay for the cost of educating a child with a disability at a private school or facility [substitute here "any services unilaterally provided"] if that school district provided a free appropriate public education…."[81] Further, "the right of reimbursement is not automatic or open-ended."[82] "Reimbursement is warranted only where, after the hearing, it is determined that the services offered by the school district are inadequate or inappropriate, the services selected by the parents are appropriate and equitable considerations support the parents' claim."[83] In New York, the "burden of proof in an administrative hearing challenging an IEP is properly placed upon the Local Education Agency (District). However, the parents bear the burden of persuasion that the program/services they provided were appropriate and reasonably calculated to enable the student to receive educational benefits.

In this instance, the CSE met their obligation to provide a FAPE by

---

80   Board of Education v. Rowley, 458 U.S. 176 [1982]

81   20 U.S.C.§1412(a)(10)(c)(iii)(I)(aa); 34 C.F.R.§300.403[d], [e][4]

82   Board of Education of the City School District of New York v. Gustafson; WL 313798 (S.D.N.Y. 2002)

83   20 U.S.C. §1412 (a)(10)(C)(ii); 34 C.F.R. §300.403(c)

developing an appropriate IEP on June 14, 2007.[84] The CSE held two additional CSE, IEP development, meetings in 2007-2008 and based their decisions for additional/revised services, on updated reports of student progress and CSE consideration of information shared by District personnel and the Parent. The IEP for the 2007-2008 school year and subsequent amendments to that IEP recommended a comprehensive program designed to ensure that the student's individual management and academic needs would be met. Therefore, it is determined that the student was offered FAPE for 2007-2008.

Having determined that Respondent met their burden of proving that the 2007-2008 IEP is appropriate and the student was provided a free appropriate public education (FAPE), the necessary inquiry is at an end and there is no need to determine that the services provided by the parent were appropriate or whether equitable considerations support Petitioner's claim.

<u>ORDER</u>

It is therefore ordered that:

1: The IEP for the 2007-2008 school year is appropriate and provided the student with a free appropriate public education (FAPE) in the least restrictive environment (LRE).

2: The parents' request for reimbursement for tutoring services unilaterally provided to the student and for reimbursement of the evaluation is denied.

3: A CSE Meeting should be convened no later than December 23, 2007, to review:

- Current status of remedial reading intervention for the student (Wilson or other);

- Updated present levels of performance (particularly in areas of reading);

---

84   Ex. D3

- Assistive technology evaluation (if not already completed and reviewed by CSE);

- Transition Plan update to include specific activities and timelines (if not already completed and reviewed by CSE); and,

- Updated annual goals to ensure that they reflect any revisions made to the IEP and reflect the student's most current functioning levels.

Dated: November 22, 2008

Mrs. Orange, Ed.D. November 22, 2008

Impartial Hearing Officer

PLEASE TAKE NOTICE

Within 30 days of receipt of this decision the parent and/or the Board of Education has a right to appeal the decision to the State Review Officer of the New York State Education Department under Section 4404 of the Education Law and the Individuals with Disabilities Act. Failure to file this notice of intention to seek review is a waiver of the right to appeal this decision.

APPENDIX C
APPEAL PETITION (12/18/08)

NEW YORK STATE EDUCATION DEPARTMENT OFFICE OF STATE REVIEW

In the Matter of the Appeal of Mr. and Mrs. Mellon, on behalf of Blake, a Student with a Disability, *Petitioner,*

-against-

SCHOOL DISTRICT, *Respondent.*

ANSWER

Petitioners, Mr. and Mrs. Mellon, as Parents of Blake, by their attorneys, LAW OFFICE OF ANDREW K. CARTER, for their petition hereby state:

1: Blake was born in 1992 and, at the outset of this impartial hearing, was attending the tenth grade.

2: His classification as a student with a learning disability is not in dispute.

3: Blake was diagnosed with developmental dyslexia, a specific learning disability in reading, by Dr. X, a neuropsychologist. Parent Ex. P-D.

4: In an evaluation conducted on January 19, 2007, Dr. X found that Blake's "history of reading and spelling difficulty and his current pattern of weaknesses are consistent with a diagnosis of Developmental Dyslexia (ICD Code 784.61).

His difficulties in the area of reading are also consistent with a diagnosis of Reading Disorder (DSM-IV-TR, Code 315.00). In addition, he shows weaknesses in the area of writing, including difficulties with grammar, syntax, and development of ideas." *Id.*, at 13.

5: Blake is nonetheless "an intellectually capable student"; his dyslexia "significantly im- pede[s] his ability to achieve up to his potential in school." *Id.*, at 14.

6: As his "learning disability has not been successfully remediated," and "he has advanced on in his academic career without having established a firm foundation in reading," his "problems with reading and written expression impact every class he takes in school." *Id.* He requires daily one-to-one reading instruction with special education teachers who are sensitive to the learning issues of an adolescent/ young adult learner.

7: In reading, the intervention should focus on making Blake's knowledge and application of phonics to word decoding more accurate as well as automatic, in order to help him to achieve mastery and automaticity when he reads. Test results revealed weaknesses in Blake's com- mand of the rules and principles of phonics, which need to be remediated in to improve his reading accuracy. The intervention should enhance his basic decoding skills, as well as increase his automaticity when reading by building his store of sight words. Focus on the rules for decoding vowel sounds will also be important, as this was identified as an area of particular weakness for Blake. The use of a systematic, phonologically-based, individualized reading program, such as the Orton-Gillingham system, which focuses on the recognition of letter patterns and whole words via drills or games, should be employed with Blake. Blake's remedial reading specialist is advised to start back at the beginning with Blake, to ensure that gaps in his phonological knowledge are filled;

this must be done sensitively so as not to embarrass Blake, who needs to be part of the team process and have a good understanding of his need for certain interventions. *Id.*, at 15.

8: He would also "benefit from receiving assistance directed at helping him to develop his higher-order reading comprehension skills. With regard to reading comprehension, Blake shows a relative weakness in his ability to grasp material at a more abstract, inferential level. Blake should be taught ways of previewing a chapter prior to reading, such as scanning chapter headings to get an overview of the content, making an outline to serve as a guide, taking down key words and short notes, and highlighting critical material as he reads." *Id.*

9: He needs to learn "learning basic spelling rules and word families, which may serve as mnemonics as he tries to remember the spelling of words." *Id.*

10: He should be be taught a "process approach to writing, which breaks down writing into its component parts." *Id.*

11: Dr. X also recommended various assistive technologies, and an assistive technology evaluation. *Id.*, at 16.

12: A copy of Dr. X's report was provided to the school district's committee on special education (CSE) prior to Blake's annual review for the 2007–08 school year. Parent Ex. P-B-2; Tr. 86–87 (Rice).

13: Mrs. Rice, the district's special education chairperson, commented that "they are good instruments that were used [by Dr. X], I believe, that the credibility of the instruments that were used and the information that they provided. What I may have some difficulty agreeing with would be the ability for a comprehensive public high school to implement some of [Dr. X's] recommendations." Tr. 92.

14: Rice believed that providing one-on-one service would be "difficult"; she also opined that the Wilson program would serve Blake's needs. Tr. 94; see also 1103 (X: Wilson would be consistent with her report).

15: According to assistant principal Mr. Jack:

> Q Do you recall Dr. X's recommendation that Blake's reading instruction be provided individually to him?
>
> A I did see that in the neuropsych, if that's what you're referring to.
>
> Q And was there any discussion providing Wilson Reading instruction to him on an individual basis?
>
> A Nobody was against it. Tr. 678.

16: While district staffers insisted that a Wilson program was offered to, and rejected by, the parents, no such program appears on any individualized education program (IEP), nor was provided at any time to Blake. See Parent Ex. P-B, P-B-1, P-B-2, P-B-3, P-B-4, P-B-5.

17: The most recent 2007–08 IEP, created at a meeting held on November 9, 2007, provides resource room for 44 minutes five days per six-day cycle, and a 15:1 social studies class for 44 minutes daily. Parent Ex. P-B.

18: It also offers books on CD, preferential seating, use of a word processor and various testing accommodations. *Id.*

19: Nowhere does it mention Wilson; while Rice testified that Wilson would only appear in the goals, and perhaps in the rationale, she admitted that the IEP goals "would be different than they are now" if Blake was to receive Wilson. Tr. 744–45.

20: On February 12, 2008, the parents requested an impartial due process hearing. Parent Ex. P-A.

21: The parents alleged failure to provide a free appropriate public education (FAPE), by declining to offer Blake specially-designed instruction in reading or math, by failing to accurately describe Blake's present levels of performance in his IEP, and by failing to provide resource room on a daily basis. The hearing request also alleged a failure to consider Dr. X's evaluation report, failure to conduct the recommended assistive technology evaluation in a timely fashion, failure to provide appropriate classroom and testing accommodations, failure to implement an appropriate transition plan, failure to provide appropriate, measurable annual goals, and failure to provide appropriate summer programming. *Id.*

22: The parents requested, *inter alia,*

- Annulment of the current IEP.

- Provision of an appropriate IEP, developed with the equal participation of the Parents and consideration of Dr. X's neuropsychological evaluation and the herein referenced AT evaluation. The IEP shall address Blake's academic, social, emotional and physical management needs. Current, accurate PLEPs (including the diagnosis of dyslexia and other diagnoses as indicated in the herein referenced evaluation) shall be included. Necessary methodologies, appropriate, measurable goals to address the needs indicated, and an appropriate transition plan shall be developed and reflected on the IEP.

- Provision of an assistive technology evaluation, and implementation of recommendations as well as goals to address those recommendations.

- Provision of the Wilson Reading Program, by an experienced individual certified and qualified Level II or trainer, of the Parent's choosing, for a minimum of one hour daily at the convenience of the family.

- Provision of extended school day academic intervention services to remediate all content areas. The District shall pay for the continuation of the current tutor's services.

- Provision of an intensive extended school year reading program of the Parent's choosing

- Reimbursement for the reading instruction that the Parents paid for privately.

- Reimbursement for the academic tutoring that the Parents paid for privately.

- Reimbursement for the independenet neuropsychological evaluation that the Parents paid for privately.

- Development of an appropriate plan of transition that includes goals and objectives and ser- vices designed to assist the student in achieving those goals and objectives. *Id.*

23: The district appointed Orange as impartial hearing officer.

24: Hearing commenced on May 1, 2008, and continued on May 5th, 14th and 20th, June 12th and 23rd, August 12th and 27th, and concluded on October 7th; the final transcript contained 1552 pages.

25: For some reason, the school district elected to elicit substantial testimony concerning approximately 331 pages of electronic mail that it submitted as exhibits. (A computer search of the record indicates that the terms "e-mail" and "email" occur on approximately 575 lines of the transcript's 1552 pages; in contrast, "Wilson," which went to the merits, occurs on just 483 lines).

26: By decision and order dated November 22, 2008, IHO Orange found:

>   1. The IEP for the 2007-2008 school year is appropriate and provided the student with a free appropriate public education (FAPE) in the least restrictive environment (LRE).
>
>   2. The parents' request for reimbursement for tutoring services unilaterally provided to the stu- dent and for reimbursement of the evaluation is denied.
>
>   3. A CSE Meeting should be convened no later than December 23, 2007.

27: See Current status of remedial reading intervention for the student (Wilson or other); Updated present levels of performance (particularly in areas of reading); Assistive technology evaluation (if not already completed and reviewed by CSE); Transition Plan update to include specific activities and timelines (if not already completed and reviewed by CSE); and, Updated annualgoalstoensurethattheyreflectanyrevisionsmadetotheIEPandreflect the student's most current functioning levels.

The IHO erred in finding that the district offered a Wilson Reading program to the stu- Parent Ex. P-B, P-B-1, P-B-2, P-B-3, P-B-4, P-B-5; Tr. 744–45. Essentially, the district staff testified that the CSE "offered" or "recommended" the Wilson reading program, but that the program was rejected by the parents. Tr. 37, 39–40, 94, 728–29 (Rice); 187 (Manna); 408, 414, 416, 437–39, 445–47, 555 (Jack); 770–72 (House); 847–49, 876–78 (Lackey). Faced with numerous federal cases requiring that the IHO limit her evaluation of a school district's "offer" to the written IEP itself, IHO Orland resorted to relying upon the comment section of the IEP, which stated that the parent had rejected a verbal offer of Wilson. The IHO clearly erred in interpreting the comment section as an "offer" of Wilson as a matter of law. Simply put, all agreed that the student needed Wilson or a similar program, and said program was not provided.

28: The IHO erred in failing to find a denial of FAPE despite her finding that the 2007/08 annual goals in reading were deficient.

29: The IHO erred in failing to consider the second prong of the *Burlington* test, namely whether the parental placement was appropriate.

30: The IHO also erred in failing to determine whether equitable reimbursement was appropriate, and in failing to grant said reimbursement.

31: The IHO erred in finding the 2007/08 IEP to be appropriate.

32: The IHO erred in failing to determine that the district should reimburse the parents for Dr. X's evaluation.

WHEREFORE, Petitioners Mr. and Mrs. Mellon respectfully requests that the Office of State Review sustain their appeal, and grant such further relief as the State Review Officer deems just and proper.

Dated: December 18, 2008

Attorneys for Respondents

Andrew K. Carter and Jason H. Stein

APPENDIX D
APPEAL DENIED (1/9/09)

I am only including the last paragraph, since it is mostly a reiteration of the earlier decision:

Finally, I note that the impartial hearing officer's decision demonstrates that she carefully marshaled and weighed all of the testimonial and documentary evidence presented by both parties with regard to the parents' procedural and substantive challenges to the student's 2007-08 IEP and properly based her ultimate determinations on the weight of the evidence. The hearing record amply supports the impartial hearing officer's conclusion that the district offered the student a program that was appropriate to meet his special education needs. In short, based upon my review of the entire hearing record, I find that the impartial hearing was conducted in a manner consistent with the requirements of due process and that there is no need to modify the findings or fact or conclusions of law as determined by the impartial hearing officer regarding the issues raised in the patents' appeal and the, the parents' appeal is dismissed in its entirety.

I have considered the parties' remaining contentions and fin that in light of my determinations, I need not reach them.

THE APPEAL IS DISMISSED.

Albany, NY January 30, 2009 State Review Officer

APPENDIX E

REFERENCES

Everyone Reading, NYC (Success for students with dyslexia & LD)

    (Formerly IDA – NY)

    www.everyonereading.org

    71 W. 23rd St, Suite 1527

    NY, NY 10010

    (212) 691-1930

International Dyslexia Association (IDA)

    www.interdys.org

    40 York Rd., 4th Floor

    Baltimore, MD 21204

    (410) 296-0232

Wilson Language Training

    www.wilsonlanguage.com

    47 Old Webster Road

    Oxford, MA 01540

    (800) 899-8454

Elaine Mellon

    unrealeducation@gmail.com

    www.unrealeducation.com

About the Author

Elaine Mellon holds a Master of Science/Certificate of Advanced Study (MS/CAS) in Counseling with a concentration in School Counseling. Her Bachelor of Arts (BA) degree is in Sociology with a minor in Psychology. Elaine has been an active and enthusiastic volunteer throughout her children's school years. For two years she was a PTA President, a Girl Scout Leader for six and held various other key positions in her children's district.

Elaine has an understanding of special education both academically and through personal experience. She learned the basic foundation in her graduate studies, but ongoing research and advanced training became imperative so she could actively and effectively advocate for her son. She accomplished this by reading, attending workshops and seminars including those online, and participating in conferences.

Married and the mother of three grown children, Elaine passionately works as a group fitness instructor, personal trainer, talent manager and travel agent.

Through this book, Elaine is hoping others will be helped, encouraged and supported as they navigate their way through the educational system, becoming a stronger, more effective and efficient advocate for their children.